THE QUIET REVOLUTION

THE QUIET REVOLUTION

Shattering the Myths about the American Criminal Justice System

ED BARAJAS

TRUE DIRECTIONS
AN AFFILIATE OF TARCHER BOOKS | iUniverse®

THE QUIET REVOLUTION
SHATTERING THE MYTHS ABOUT THE
AMERICAN CRIMINAL JUSTICE SYSTEM

iUniverse books may be ordered through booksellers or by contacting:

iUniverse
1663 Liberty Drive
Bloomington, IN 47403
www.iuniverse.com
1-800-Authors (1-800-288-4677)

ISBN: 978-1-4917-4900-5 (sc)
ISBN: 978-1-4917-4901-2 (hc)
ISBN: 978-1-4917-4899-2 (e)

Library of Congress Control Number: 2014917547

Printed in the United States of America.

iUniverse rev. date: 11/3/2014

To my beautiful wife, Barbara. She's been my inspiration, ally, and muse throughout the process. If not for her, I may never have taken this step.

Although this book is about the criminal justice system in general, this is also to our nation's correctional officers, who work unarmed and unafraid among some of the worst offenders in our country.

PREFACE

I wrote this book primarily out of frustration. After years of reading about or watching and reading news stories about the need to reform our criminal justice system from the point of view of the reformer's narrative, I decided to take action. After working twenty-seven years within the correctional system at various levels, I knew that the message about what was really wrong with the system wasn't getting out.

I've worked in some capacity with all the justice components, but I began my criminal justice education as a young, idealistic, and naïve correctional officer in a federal penitentiary. As I progressed through the system, I changed my thinking but not my principles. I owe a large part of that transformation to the great bunch of men (it was all male back then) of the "custodial" force of correctional officers at the McNeil Island Federal Penitentiary.

In the 1995 movie *Heat*, Lt. Vincent Hanna, played by Al Pacino, confronts bank robber Neil McCuley, played by Robert De Niro. Hanna says to McCauley, "Seven years in Folsom. In the hole for three. McNeil before that. McNeil as tough as they say?"

I found myself feeling a twinge of pride at the mention of the place where I learned and gained so much.

If it was as tough as they say, it wasn't because of harsh treatment from the correctional officers. They went about their thankless tasks with professionalism and dignity. Between the occasional moments of alarm and confrontations with disruptive inmates were months of peaceful interactions between staff and prisoners.

These officers never became demoralized. Part of the reason for this was because of the bonds of camaraderie we formed through our shared and lack-of-acclaim jobs. Maybe it's because many officers were retired from the military, were more mature in years and experience, or I'm just biased, but the correctional officer force at McNeil Island was among the best, if not *the* best, I saw throughout my career. I'm proud to have been a part of not only the McNeil Island staff but also the Bureau of Prisons staff.

The McNeil Island prison is now long gone. In 1981, the BOP turned over operations to Washington State, and McNeil Island became a state prison. In 2011, it closed for good, marking the end of an era.

I mention this because, of all the justice components targeted by reformers, the prison system is the most maligned. Prisons are portrayed in a negative light in most, if not all, accounts available to the public. Prison guards are always portrayed as not much better, if not altogether worse, than the inmates.

There are many of us who know better, but our voices are never heard.

INTRODUCTION

I've never been one for moral equivalence, that insidious politically correct malady that seems to permeate contemporary culture. It seems to infuse everything from domestic and foreign policy to politics, religion, and education. The idea is that there's no such thing as moral superiority. All actions are equally moral, whether it's the stoning of women for adultery or blocking their advancement by a glass ceiling. Oppression is the same, no matter what form it takes or whatever the reasons.

This may seem like an unconventional way of beginning a book about criminal justice, but I think it's appropriate given the nature of the bulk of available information regarding the system.

It once was easy to identify the "bad guys" and to distinguish them from the "good guys." Now it looks as if there's neither, and what remains is a feeble brand of amoral sentimentality. When it comes to criminal justice, what tends to get published and reported is from the perspective of people who hold the system in contempt and view offenders as it's victims. The real victims, those who are preyed upon and terrorized by criminals in the system, are seldom mentioned. Not much is written about or reported from their point of view.

Some people in our country have developed a strategy of calling for reform of our institutions and policies by portraying our current course of action as inherently malicious. This applies not only to all of our domestic and foreign policies in general but to our criminal justice system and policies in particular.

We constantly read and are told that our country has the highest incarceration rate in the world and that our criminal justice system is rife with injustice and bigotry. This implies some type of racist police state because our premier incarceration rate in the world is more oppressive than countries like North Korea and Iran.

Therefore, who are we to judge other countries for their harsh punishment practices? Doesn't an examination of our criminal justice system reveal as many, if not more, human rights violations? The subliminal message is that our system must be reformed because it's more vindictive toward its citizens than even the world's most repressive regimes. It's therefore broken and doesn't work. But is this true?

The same experts that tout this line appear to be baffled at the most important social trend of the past twenty years: the United States' plunging crime rate. The facts tell us that instead of a broken system, something appears to be working.

The homicide rate fell 51 percent between 1993 and 2012 from 9.5 per 100,000 residents to 4.7 per 100,000. Property crime also fell sharply during that time. Auto theft, a persistent scourge of urban life, dropped an astounding 62 percent.[1] It's likely that these trends will continue into the future.

Americans also report being less fearful of crime. Three decades ago, according to Gallup, 48 percent of Americans said they feared walking alone at night within a mile of their homes.[2] On May 15, 2013, Jim Clifton, chairman of Gallup, reported that 25 percent of Americans feared walking alone in their neighborhoods.[3] The fear factor had been cut almost in half.

Most criminal justice experts are at a loss to explain the precise causes of crime's decline. Some observations defy conventional wisdom, such as lower crime in the middle of tough economic conditions. Increasing incarceration gives a partial explanation. But crime rates continued to fall after December 31, 2008, when incarceration peaked at about 1.6 million.[4]

It seems clear that many have underestimated Americans' capacity to tackle a seemingly uncontrollable problem and fix it. For the past twenty years, there's been a quiet revolution occurring in criminal justice seemingly beyond the view, and perhaps the grasp, of many experts. What's at the heart of the remarkable drop in crime is the transition from the traditional criminal justice system whose focus is on doing things *to* or *for* offenders to a new criminal justice model dedicated to collaboration with citizens, victims, and other criminal justice components in an effort to create and maintain safer communities.

In 1995, I wrote a paper, "Moving toward Community Justice," describing the revolutionary changes taking place in criminal justice. These changes were the beginning of a seismic shift in the way the system operated and how it viewed its mission. I've observed these changes during twenty-seven years as a corrections practitioner with the Federal Bureau of Prisons and the National Institute of Corrections.

These changes continue to shape and improve the justice system, but many people who are considered criminal justice experts don't seem to grasp this reality. They would much rather persist with endless complaints about the abusive and unjust nature of our justice system and present their own misguided and misdirected solutions. They represent the criminal justice reform movement, which has taken on a life of its own with endless condemnations of our system. It's not that our justice system doesn't need to change and improve—quite the contrary, it's that the reform movement uses a false narrative to advance its objectives.

The criminal justice reform narrative goes something like this: Our criminal justice system is the most punitive in the world as evidenced by our country having the highest incarceration rate in the world. Our prisons are filled with a high number of low-level, nonviolent offenders who should not be locked up. Not only are prisons severely overcrowded, but also they don't work. High recidivism rates indicate that prisons make people worse, especially all of those low-level offenders. Our prison system is too expensive and threatens to bankrupt our states while taking money away from such vital things as education for our children. We must therefore establish "smarter" sentencing plus alternatives to incarceration instead of the "lock 'em up and throw away the key" mentality of our current system.

The narrative is reflected in the titles of books that call for changing the system, such as *Our Punitive Society: Race, Class, Gender and Punishment in America*; *Punishment and Inequality in America*; and *The Punishment Imperative: The Rise and Failure of Mass Incarceration*. This reflects the type of information disseminated by academia among students, criminal justice organizations, and the general public. The ultimate goal is to influence the policy-making structures of government at all levels.

The types of books reflected in the above titles were the tools of my learning, or indoctrination, as a college sociology/criminology major. They and the general atmosphere of the late 1960s and early 1970s in colleges across America instilled in me a certain righteous indignation and a desire to try to right the wrongs of "the system" against the poor and other oppressed minorities. According to the established narrative, these oppressed minorities were to be found disproportionately in our nation's prisons. I thus set out, as many others did, to join the justice reform movement. As a

Mexican American, this seeming injustice affected me on a very personal level. I was motivated to start a sort of revolution from within the prison system, and this was one reason for my choice of employment.

In college, I had been taught the usual truisms about prisons and our criminal justice system. Accounts about justice in America were filled with horror stories about the gross unfairness of our system and the brutality and harshness of our prisons. As my work experience expanded through various functions within federal prisons, community corrections, and policy-influencing organizations at the national level, my awareness expanded progressively and shattered the myths, which had been taught to me as truth and influenced by the popular revolutionary fervor of the times.

Nonetheless, these myths persist to this day and are firmly entrenched among the highest circles of academia and certain criminal justice organizations. For decades, an entire industry of offender advocates, who are considered criminal justice experts, has taken up the banner of justice reform and is engaged in the movement of providing policymakers answers to what I believe are the wrong questions and implementing solutions to what I believe are the wrong problems. Much of what the public has been exposed to regarding the criminal justice system is the product of this movement and the perpetuation of these myths.

This book is my opportunity to set the record straight about the true nature of the problems of the criminal justice system and what needs to be done to address them. I want to add to the title of books transmitting the reform narrative, a book written from actual experience in the trenches dealing with the everyday problems of the system. I want to shatter the prism of dogmatic, established thinking within the criminal justice reform movement that has little regard for opposing views.

This book is not intended to be an academic tome. I think of it more as a primer about our criminal justice system. It's a to-the-point, quick-and-dirty description of the problems it faces and addresses. I'll also describe the improvements that have occurred and are occurring.

In this book I will address:

- The confusion regarding the overall mission of the criminal justice system, especially as it relates to public safety.
- I'll dispel some of the most prevalent myths regarding this system and point out some of the vital questions that are never asked to reformers by policymakers.

- I'll provide a history of how the justice system got into its present predicament as well as some of the truly revolutionary practices that are improving the system by not merely *reforming* it but by *transforming* it.

Throughout the book, I refer to offender advocates, experts or criminal justice experts, and the (criminal justice) reform movement, or reformers. For all practical purposes, they refer to a movement and the individuals within it who believe our country is much too harsh on our treatment of offenders. An anti-incarceration fervor that views prisons as a necessary evil at best and a shameful institution at worst drives the movement. Its energy is focused on influencing public perception and to shape public policy regarding our criminal justice system.

The criminal justice system is experiencing the same sense of awakening I had during my career and consequently is becoming more effective and efficient. Crime rates have been steadily declining over the past two decades. Judging from the latest media articles and interviews, justice reform experts are clueless regarding why. I suggest the reason for this decline in crime is not because of the loud voices of the decades-old justice reform movement but rather because of a growing, transformational, quiet revolution. It is a quiet revolution that seems to have escaped the notice of the news media and criminal justice reform advocates. The change is dedicated to public safety, security, and community quality of life.

During my time as a correctional program specialist at the NIC, I would visit various jurisdictions and would often be introduced as a criminal justice expert. I would respond that I wasn't an expert. Experts have all the answers. My job was to help them ask all the right questions. This is how good policy formulation begins. Most, if not all, of what we consider failed or bad policy is the direct result of ignoring this crucial first step. This crucial step in criminal justice policy formulation is often ignored because the justice reform movement and its anointed experts are intolerant of imposing and opposing questions and opinions. In this book, I'll ask and provide those questions and opinions.

I should add that during the writing of this book the unrest in Ferguson, Missouri, erupted after the shooting by police of an unarmed African-American man. This brought up the question of another change occurring in many police departments.

Police departments have been expanding their SWAT teams and obtaining surplus military hardware. The inevitable question of whether the "militarization" of the police is good or bad for police practices has arisen. This is a crucial and legitimate question but one that isn't the focus of this book.

To adequately answer the question would probably require another volume devoted solely to that topic.

The criminal justice system does need to change and improve. Although positive changes are happening, much remains to be done. The corrections system in particular suffers from a sort of identity crisis that makes it tone deaf, if not altogether hostile, to the demands of the public. The correctional system often views the public as a hindrance to its mission rather than the focus of its efforts.

Because of this, it's the best place to begin this book with the most basic question of all.

CHAPTER 1

Who Are Our Customers?

"F _ _ _ them! Who do they think they are?"

After working several years in prisons and other correctional settings I'm not easily offended or shocked by foul language. In this case however I was taken aback by the source of the comment. I had recently been assigned to the National Institute of Corrections (NIC) in Washington DC. A workshop participant at an American Probation and Parole Association (APPA) conference uttered that indignant statement—similar to several others regarding the workshop topic of expanding the use of community corrections centers (halfway houses) as a sentencing option.

The discussion was focused on the personal experiences of the workshop participants who were employees or directors of these facilities. Someone talked about the neighborhood residents surrounding his facility and their complaints about the facility's residents hanging outside the center at night and making too much noise. They had suggested that the facility institute some type of curfew to ensure that all the occupants were inside after certain hours.

The angry responses spoke volumes. My immediate reaction to the question "Who do they think they are?" was to think what I assumed was obvious. "They" were the people that paid our salaries. In other words, they were the people we served and should be the focus of our concern for their safety and well-being.

This lack of concern for the public interest sums up what ails the justice system in general and the corrections system in particular. The system has lost sight of what its mission is and whom it is they serve. Like the participants in this workshop, individuals within the criminal justice reform movement perceive themselves as experts in their fields who don't need advice from an ill-informed public. What good is trying to expand "community" corrections when the community is considered with such disregard and even contempt? This is one question that never enters the minds of these "experts" and a concept they can't seem to grasp.

In articles, studies, and speeches by these experts, the public is portrayed as akin to a lynch mob hell-bent on revenge. According to this view, the public is behind the tough-on-crime policies that have resulted in mass incarceration. It therefore follows that politicians, more concerned about reelection than public service, have submitted to the will of the mob and passed ever-more punitive legislation. This results in more harm to what are referred to as "our clients" (the offenders) who are supposed to be the sole focus of our concern and efforts.

The public, on the other hand, generally thinks that the correctional system consists of only prisons or jails. They tend to view prisons as either too harsh or too lenient (i.e. "country club" prisons). Because of the system's sole focus on offenders and the attitudes of many corrections professionals, they believe that the system is indeed a "criminal" justice system. Justice is only considered for the criminal and not for victims or the communities they harm.

While at NIC, I worked to counteract this mind-set and to try refocusing the mission of corrections to the public interest and public safety. Questions needed to be asked in order to transform the justice and corrections systems. What was the purpose and value of corrections? Who or what is the main focus of concern?

I wanted to work with crime-victim-related issues. I always believed that victims were forgotten or ignored by the criminal justice system. When my coworkers found out what I wanted to focus on, one of them asked me if I really wanted to work with "damn victims." My belief was proven correct.

If the system considers the general public as something akin to an ill- informed lynch mob, victims drive and energize the mob. The system considers them useful only in terms of being witnesses for the prosecution. After they fulfill that role, they're all but forgotten and have to fend for themselves.

This view of victims has begun to change for the better but needs more work. Pressure from victims' rights and certain reform groups has forced many corrections departments, prosecutors, and courts to establish victims' assistance programs. This is a great step in the right direction but needs more work. Victims' assistance needs to become embedded within the system's common mission rather than one of its many tasks.

The disregard for victims is most often not intentional but a result of the blind side within operating practices of the organization's mission. In other words, when the sole focus of the work is the offender, all other matters seem to become fuzzy or simply disappear.

I once was asked to speak to a class at Georgetown University Law Center. The instructor was a former head of community corrections in a state corrections department at about the same time I had been a community corrections manager in Seattle for the BOP. He began class by asking me how many times one of my clients had murdered a member of the community during their stay in one of the community facilities I oversaw. I responded that, thankfully, no such incidents had occurred.

He seemed to be taken aback by my response and was temporarily silent. He then told the class that this was unusual because during the time he was assigned to community corrections at the state level, three such murders had occurred. He went on to say that this was the terrible but necessary price that must be paid in our efforts to rehabilitate offenders. I was astonished at the matter-of-fact manner of his statement. I had to take a deep breath before I spoke.

I then went on to explain that the BOP placed a high premium on public safety above all else. We would not and did not hesitate to remove anyone from a community facility and send him back to prison for the slightest infraction if we thought the individual would present a great risk to the public. He responded that in his experience reducing recidivism was the main goal. They gave offenders several chances before they sent them back to prison, and the offense had to be very serious.

"Like killing someone?" I asked.

"Well, yes," he responded.

I don't know if he was aware of the senseless irony of his statement. Three innocent victims had been murdered because of this insane policy. Unfortunately, that reflects the nature of corrections in our country. In an effort to reduce recidivism, a direct but unfortunate by-product is that innocent people are essentially murdered.

One of my first assignments at NIC was to help develop a mission statement for community corrections. I was at a meeting of several heads of probation and parole agencies to discuss ideas and to develop a work plan. After a discussion regarding the lack of public support and understanding, I suggested that we begin describing what defines the work of community corrections by some type of value statement—something that states the "so what" of what we do. I suggested something like "Community corrections contributes to or promotes public safety by ..."

The response was silence followed by several people telling me that public safety was not the goal of community corrections. I was stunned and thought to myself that these people shouldn't wonder why the public didn't support them. I asked them what the goal of the work was, and they responded that it was to affect positive change in offenders.

While I strongly support rehabilitation efforts, I believe that rehabilitation is one means to an end. The end must be public safety, and all the criminal justice components should work in concert toward this end.

In most of academia and at the highest levels of criminal justice agencies, the belief is that the true purpose of the system should be rehabilitation. Tougher sentencing laws are seen as attempts to force the system to punish rather than rehabilitate offenders. The mistaken message is that in order to do one you should stop doing the other. What's lost in translation is that rehabilitation and punishment are actually two sides of the same coin—the offender. The endless debate is on what to do *to* them or *for* them.

This primary focus on the needs (for punishment or rehabilitation) of the offender is why we've never had an effective crime policy in this country. I participated in countless discussions and workshops in Washington DC, where everyone thought we were discussing crime, but in fact we were discussing individual criminal behavior. The discussion was always about how best to respond to offenders *after* they commit a crime.

Criminal behavior concerns the micro, or individual deviant acts that bring people into the system. Crime is the macro, or large-scale community environment in which those individual actions occur and thus affect the safety and well-being of the public at large. This is similar to the differences between individual sickness and illness on the one hand and general health on the other. Improvements in the medical profession have started focusing more on maintaining health (macro) rather than only treating illness after a person gets sick (micro).

We constantly debate on whether to get meaner and harsher or kinder and gentler on what we do to or for offenders. If we were to focus on the best means of creating safer communities, we might begin to realize that the types of services and supervision provided to offenders are a means to an end rather the purpose of the work. The ultimate end should be public safety.

The justice system is a system in name only. It doesn't have a common, overarching mission or common principles among its components of the police, prosecution, courts, and corrections. About the only common thing they share is a focus on apprehending and processing individual offenders within each individual part.

In traditional policing, the police apprehend lawbreakers and process their arrests. The prosecution processes them for conviction. The courts process them through trial, conviction, and sentencing, and corrections carries out their sentencing. The common function is to process cases throughout the system. All of these processes occur after a crime has been committed, so there's very little emphasis on crime prevention. Because the system's primary concern is on apprehending and processing "the bad guys," the rights and needs of victims are all but ignored.

This sole or primary focus on the offender is ingrained within the framework of the system and was further enhanced in the turbulent times of the early 1970s.

The National Institute of Corrections (NIC) was established in the wake of the 1971 Attica Prison uprising in upstate New York that shook the nation's conscience about the state of America's prisons. Attorney General John N. Mitchell convened a national conference on corrections in Williamsburg, Virginia. A federal agency within the US Justice Department and within, but autonomous from, the organizational structure of the Federal Bureau of Prisons (BOP) was established and charged with providing training and technical assistance to state and local corrections departments. Many seem to have seen this as a mandate for a "kinder, gentler" corrections system, meaning a sole focus on more attention and services for offenders.

Due in large part to the efforts of various criminal justice organizations, as well as the reform-minded history of prisons in America, most state corrections systems view their mission as rehabilitating offenders. This is true even in states that have enacted "punitive get tough" measures. The American penitentiary is a product of reform by Philadelphia Quakers. They wanted to reform or "correct" offenders through penance. The ultimate result was a system of corrections through reformatories and penitentiaries. Some state corrections departments operate under the state departments of social services. This is why within these agencies there's hostility against what they consider to be an ill-informed public interfering with their true mission of rehabilitation.

This may seem contradictory because the prison reform movement's primary objection is that prisons fail to rehabilitate offenders. The great irony is that many people in the highest echelons of corrections share this opinion and are sympathetic to the reform movement's objectives. They view the public's demand to "get tough on crime" as the greatest impediment toward this goal.

At NIC, I directed my efforts to refocusing the work of corrections to the community and victims and on trying to get the system to function as a true system rather than as a collection of parts. My worldview had been shaped by working within an organization, the Federal Bureau of Prisons, with a clear sense of mission that collaborates with the other justice components. The organizational culture where I gained my experience was very different from the organizational cultures where my NIC colleagues had worked. Just about all my coworkers came from state and local systems. This would prove to be a source of some tension, but at the same time, I was able to learn considerably by contrasting and comparing the federal system with state and local systems.

The best place to begin to describe the BOP is in its mission statement.

> We protect public safety by ensuring that federal offenders serve their sentences of imprisonment in facilities that are safe, humane, cost-efficient, and appropriately secure, and provide reentry programming to ensure their successful return to the community.

This clearly describes the focus and value of its efforts—protecting public safety.

One thing that distinguishes the Bureau of Prisons (BOP) from most state corrections agencies is their view of staff in the overall contribution to the mission. With regard to the overall mission, all staff members are considered to be correctional officers in much the same way as everyone in the Marine Corps is considered to be an infantryman regardless of job title. All bureau staff receives identical training in firearms, search procedures, self-defense, restraints, and all other matters related to the safety and security of the institution. If a disturbance occurs, it wouldn't be unusual to see riot squads consisting of correctional officers, factory foremen, counselors, caseworkers, and even secretaries.

Most wardens and other top-level managers began their careers as correctional officers or other line staff in an institution. They were promoted through the ranks rather than being rewarded their positions through political patronage as in other state and local correctional systems.

The BOP works very closely with the other components in the justice system. As part of my job in community corrections, as well as in case management in prisons, I had to work closely with federal courts, federal probation and parole, the US Marshals Service in particular, and other federal, state, and local law enforcement in general. This cooperation and interagency collaboration made for more effective and efficient operations.

Federal judges, either directly or through federal probation officers under the federal courts, often consult with the BOP regarding sentencing recommendations to find out such things as where an offender might serve his or her sentence, the security-level facility he or she might qualify for, and other matters. The BOP considers federal probation, which is under the federal court system, its eyes and ears in the community. Probation officers write presentence investigation reports (PSIs) on all offenders entering custody.

The PSI is an invaluable tool in security-level classification consideration (from minimum to maximum security institutions) and for release planning. The report is a detailed account of the offender's current offense plus prior criminal record. It also describes the offender's family and employment history as well as any history of drug abuse or mental-health problems.

The US Marshals Service transports newly sentenced offenders to their designated corrections facilities, arrests federal probation violators and absconders, and apprehends federal escapees and fugitives. The collaboration between the US Marshals Service and the Bureau of Prisons is crucial in ensuring public safety.

Contrasting my experience with collaborative work practices of the federal system with others, I learned that the American criminal justice system is a system in name only. Not only are there no overarching, common operating principles, but also each component pretty much operates on its own within its individual management culture and perceived mandate.

The "system's" main function is to process cases within its individual parts without, or with little, regard for the whole. The ultimate purpose of the whole depends on whom you ask within this processing body. An important consideration is that policy formulation within each component depends primarily on the passage of new laws at the federal and state levels. This often causes agency directors to resist independently establishing more innovative agency operating procedures.

When I transferred to NIC, I was assigned to the community corrections department because of my experience as a community corrections manager with the BOP. I had worked in this position in Brooklyn, New York, and in Seattle, Washington. At the Seattle office, my responsibilities covered a four-state area of Washington, Oregon, Idaho, and Alaska.

As a community corrections manager, my job had been to monitor community treatment facilities, or halfway houses, as well as local jails under contract to the federal government. I was also responsible for designating newly sentenced federal offenders to specific federal institutions based on their security needs, which were determined by their sentence length, prior records, and other factors. I also had the authority to transfer inmates back to federal prison or to a local jail for disciplinary reasons.

While assigned to Seattle, a director of a community facility in Alaska called and told me that a particular federal resident was being disruptive. He refused to follow the rules and had a couple of curfew violations. I checked the man's Jacket (inmate file) and saw that he had an extensive record and a history of violence. I contacted the marshal's office in Anchorage, and within ten minutes, the man was in custody, awaiting transport back to federal prison.

The next day, the director called to thank me and said that I had put the fear of God into the residents in that facility, which consisted largely of state offenders. Whenever they violated any rules, he'd call the state authorities and was told to give them warnings. He could never get them to send anybody back to prison unless they did something really serious, and when they did return someone to custody, it was a complicated process. The federal residents thought they were operating under the same policy and thus had become cocky. This incident not only changed the federal residents' minds, but it also had an effect on the state residents as well. The facility was a lot easier to manage after that.

This focus on public safety does not and should not diminish the importance of rehabilitation and treatment programs. Reformed offenders no longer pose a threat to the community. We must realize, however, that we must strive to prevent offenders from victimizing the public either because they no longer care to or they no longer can because of tighter controls and confinement. Both are equally worthy means to an end.

The police, indeed the entire justice system, are viewed as a necessary evil by many academics and scholars. This is understandable because of the American culture and history. Our founders, ever mindful of governments' tendency to encroach on civil liberties, ensured that individual rights as well as the means to defend against the abuse of state power were codified in our constitution.

It's therefore easy to conclude that institutions that deprive individuals of their liberty are inherently evil. The drive then becomes to create justice institutions that are less harsh and punitive, and I see this as a worthy and noble effort. But the efforts focus on the wrong problem and propose the wrong solutions.

I've heard talks and speeches and have read articles by heads of corrections agencies that denounce prisons and incarceration in order to promote "alternative sentencing options." I couldn't imagine the CEO of General Motors denouncing cars in order to promote public transportation. Try to imagine the CEO of a major hospital group denouncing hospitals and hospitalization in order to promote community urgent care facilities.

That's why the health care reform debate is focused on broader issues of insurance portability, preexisting conditions, greater and less expensive coverage, etc. It isn't focused on the questions of building more or fewer hospitals. We know that hospitals and hospitalization are neither good nor bad in and of themselves. They are only one component and option within the health care system.

Unlike corrections, other professions and agencies, such as health care and private business, have a clear sense of mission and purpose. That mission is seen within a broader, common systemic purpose. Cars, as well as all other motor vehicles, are part of our country's transportation system. Hospitals, urgent care facilities, and all other related components are part of the health care system.

I don't really know why so many high-ranking corrections officials show such disregard for the very institutions they manage. I think it has to do with the political nature of appointing corrections officials in our states. I once heard an astonishing tale by a warden of a state prison. He said he had been appointed as an associate warden in a state prison soon after he retired from the military. His first day on the job was the first day he had ever been inside a prison. As he walked around, someone handed him a stack of files and told him he was in charge of inmate disciplinary hearings for that day.

In the 1990s, the appointed head of a state corrections department was a former mortician who ran a mortuary business. There's a business management philosophy founded on the principle that a manager is a manager, no matter what the business. I guess that's one justification.

That fact is that people from other disciplines bring their biased views about prisons when they're appointed. These views have been shaped by the myths fed to them by the news media and academia. It thus stands to reason that they perceive criminal justice reform as prison reform and reducing imprisonment.

The justice system in general has no common mission or purpose and each component acts semi-independently to process cases rather than to confront the public safety problems of our communities. Corrections in particular finds itself adrift in a void of self-imposed alienation suffering a perpetual identity crisis and a sense of victimization by the public and political forces. Its leaders are constantly blaming outside forces for their plight instead of looking in the mirror for someone to blame. They constantly seek to educate the public regarding the "true" mission of corrections, meaning to enlighten people about the benefits of a less-punitive system. But no one ever stops to consider that education is a two-way street, and most often, the people who need more education are corrections professionals and other "experts."

What the system needs to do is shift its focus to the community and create a public-safety model of justice. Instead of focusing on how to respond to individual acts of criminal behavior after the fact, it must look to better ways of confronting crime. In such a model, rehabilitation and punishment become two of several means rather than *the* purpose of the system.

A common mission focused on creating and maintaining safer communities would transform the system from primarily processing cases into a larger context of confronting crime by solving problems at all levels, especially at the neighborhood level, and by preventing crimes from occurring in the first place. This would be a more proactive method of crime control rather than the traditional reactive method of acting after the commission of a crime.

A public-safety model of justice would require different success measures. We've looked to recidivism as a success measure for far too long. The problem is that it's a flawed success measure because it looks at the wrong thing. Simply considering that someone hasn't returned to custody without asking why is foolish and dangerous.

We know that a person can avoid incarceration for a variety of reasons while continuing to wreak havoc in the community. If an offender is released from prison in one state and is arrested in another, the first state can claim a "successful release" simply because the individual didn't return to custody in that state. A person can be arrested multiple times with no convictions because of victim intimidation. This is considered success. Relying on recidivism as a success measure also has unintended consequences.

NIC provides training to probation and parole officers instructing them not to revoke anyone unless or until they commit a serious offense, such as murder or assault. Offenders in community programs often receive numerous warnings or are placed in other community programs deemed "more intensive." For many offenders, this is a suitable policy.

It must be pointed out that many serious offenses could be prevented by revoking certain habitual offenders, such as chronic domestic abusers, at the first sign of trouble, such as a minor violation. To do so, however, would be considered a failure in the traditional system. This makes no sense at all. For the sake of public safety, it must be understood that reducing recidivism and reducing victimization *are not* one and the same.

In short, if the purpose of the justice system is to be a gatekeeper for prisons, recidivism makes sense. If the purpose of the system is to create and maintain safer communities, it does not.

Despite these facts, which seem to be obvious to the average citizen, a faction of academic criminologists and high-ranking criminal justice officials continues to preserve and promote the reform agenda. This agenda is what drives the dialogue and is responsible for the policies that continue to alienate our citizens—the very people who must be enlisted in the work to create a better and improved justice system.

We currently have a criminal justice system focused on the needs of the individual criminal regarding punishment, rehabilitation, etc. We think in terms of what to do to or for offenders *after* they commit a crime. This is a reactive approach, which leaves little or no consideration for prevention. This sole focus on the individual offender blinds many professionals within the system to the needs of victims and the community and creates alienation with citizens.

The criminal justice system is a system in name only with each individual component working semi-independently, if not entirely independently, of the others and without a common mission, principles, and values. It processes cases rather than solves problems, and its success is measured on how many less inmates it produces rather than on how many less victims.

The reason the system needs to change is not that it's too punitive or too lenient. The purpose of change should not be to become meaner and harsher or kinder to and gentler on offenders.

We have a system of justice that responds to individual criminal acts and criminal behavior after the fact and strives to keep offenders out of prison. What we need is a justice system that confronts and prevents crime, with a shared mission to keep communities and victims safe. That is why the system must change.

Getting the justice system we need would result from a criminal justice transformation. We can never accomplish that without discarding the prevailing and persistent reform narrative.

The good news is that for the past three decades such a transformation has been occurring under the noses of the some of the system's harshest critics. The justice system is coming alive, or more specifically, being reborn with a renewed sense of purpose that puts the safety, health, and security of the community at the top of its priorities along with a genuine concern for the well-being of crime victims. The fact that most critics don't seem to have noticed this revolution means that they're either not paying attention or are more concerned with their usual business of lobbying at the political level for reform legislation.

Because the system is now progressing without their apparent knowledge and expertise, maybe they should reconsider their own operating principles and values.

CHAPTER 2

Presenting Victimizers as Victims

CRIME RATE DOWN, BUT PRISON POPULATION ON THE RISE[5]

It seems the above headline would bewilder any individual of normal intelligence. Would any journalist ever consider a headline such as: ILITERACY RATE DOWN, BUT SCHOOL POPULATION ON THE RISE? This is how the reform movement uses the news media as its messengers. They expect ill-informed rubes, otherwise known as the public, to swallow every word. Such unsophisticated readers could never wonder if the crime rate was down *because* the prison population was on the rise. Doesn't the public, after all, demand tougher sentencing because they willingly feed off of crime horror stories served by the news media?

The case must therefore be made that in this "the land of the free," our incarceration rates are the highest in the world. This shows that our justice system is harsh, vindictive, and only concerned with retribution and punishment. Because of this, our only or primary sentencing option is prison.

The public must be constantly informed that prisons and incarceration are, for the most part, useless and needless. They fail to transform thugs into responsible, law-abiding citizens. If crime rates rise, we're told that incarceration doesn't work. If crime rates drop, we're told that incarceration isn't needed. Prisons are also filled with nonviolent or low-level drug offenders or not-dangerous individuals but should only house the most violent, such as serial rapists or murderers.

It should be noted that in the worldview described by this narrative, there are two and only two points of view—those who favor rehabilitation and those who favor punishment as the purpose of the system. Reformers

13

favor the former while anyone who disagrees in any way is viewed as favoring the latter. There's no thought of considering that rehabilitation and punishment can be equally worthy means to an end—safer communities.

In 2014, a story in the Tennessean stated that interest groups from all sides of the political spectrum were advising members of the Tennessee Senate about "fixing" criminal justice in the state. The stated problem was that Tennessee needed to reduce its prison population and recidivism rate. The solution was more alternatives to incarceration.

Tennessee obviously had a problem because it locks up more people than most states and yet had the highest rate of violent crime in 2012.[6] Apparently no one bothered to ask if Tennessee locks up more people *because* it has the highest rate of violent crime. Neither did anyone ask why Tennessee needed to put more people in alternatives to incarceration when about 74 per cent of the state's corrections population is not locked up but under community supervision—in other words, alternatives to incarceration.

Nowhere in the story did it state that the purpose of fixing Tennessee's criminal justice system was to create a safer state by confronting and reducing crime, especially in view of their high violent crime rate. The focus was on reducing incarceration and recidivism.

Reformers state that we must have alternatives to incarceration for the majority of offenders. This would be a much cheaper alternative to the immensely expensive prisons that take money from education and other vital services and are draining our government budgets.

This is a winning PR strategy for the reform industry but a loser with the public at large. Reformers are extremely frustrated with the lack of huge public outcry against prisons, but they shouldn't wonder why.

In the 1980s and 1990s, the criminal justice pendulum swung to a get-tough approach to sentencing that had resulted in a binge of mass incarceration—or so we were constantly told. Supposedly, our prisons were not only dangerously overcrowded but were filled with low-level, nonviolent offenders. We needed alternatives to incarceration, and we needed to convince policymakers to start implementing them in their jurisdictions.

The resulting reform narrative became, and is, an anti-incarceration effort disguised as criminal justice reform. Every effort was focused on reducing incarceration rather than on improving the entire system. If the system was discussed at all, the discussion focused on making a systemic effort to reduce incarceration. This scenario is a constant in the criminal justice reform movement. This narrative has proven to be so dynamic that it continues to grow. The sources of the narrative used to be mostly liberal, or those on the left of the political spectrum, as well as libertarians.

This is an example from Attorney General Eric Holder speaking to the National Organization of Black Law Enforcement Executives on February 12, 2010:

> It's time to face facts about our current approach to incarceration. It's not sustainable. It's not affordable. And we've seen that it isn't always as effective as we think in reducing crime and keeping Americans safe. [7]

In the twenty-first century, more Conservatives joined their ranks. Take the following excerpt from the statement of principles from the conservative organization "Right on Crime":

> A clear example is our reliance on prisons, which serve a critical role by incapacitating dangerous offenders and career criminals but are not the solution for every type of offender. And in some instances, they have the unintended consequence of hardening nonviolent, low-risk offenders—making them a greater risk to the public than when they entered. [8]

The description of the problem and needed solutions is not supported by facts. As to the claim that all or most of what we're doing in response to crime is to lock people up, the facts look very different.

According to the Bureau of Justice Statistics (BJS), at the end of 2012, the United States had a total corrections population of 6,937,600. This included 4,781,300 under community supervision or "alternatives" (primarily probation and parole). This means that more than two-thirds of our corrections population is supervised in the community rather than locked up. In some states, the community corrections population, as community supervision is called, is more than 80 percent of the total corrections population and has been for decades.[9] This one factor alone does more to discredit the reform narrative than any other.

The problem is that most people don't know that the corrections population not only includes probation and parole but also comprises the largest segment of the corrections system. They only hear about the small percentages that are in prison. The public may therefore become susceptible to claims that incarceration is our only or primary option. When reformers demand that we place more offenders in "alternatives to incarceration," they're basically demanding that the system do what it's already doing and has been doing for decades.

This has created one of the greatest ironies. In their attempts to sell community corrections to the public, the experts have managed to convince the American people that community corrections doesn't exist.

In order to understand the real problem with our justice system, it's important to examine the various myths of the reform narrative. I believe that the following seven are the most prevalent and therefore most important to dispel.

Myth #1: Poverty causes crime.

We're constantly told through news articles and other sources that poverty causes crime. This makes intuitive sense. Most of the crime that frightens most Americans are the street crimes of muggings, gang-related shootings, and other activities. Most of these crimes occur in certain inner-city neighborhoods in the poorest sections of town. We're told that people who are deprived by society for opportunities to succeed legitimately have little choice but to turn to illegitimate means of survival. At least that's what I was taught in college.

Although most crime is associated with certain parts of communities, this doesn't mean that the poverty of these communities is the cause. In fact, according to a study by James K. Stewart, former director of the National Institute of Justice, it's the other way around. Crime causes poverty. According to the study conducted in 1986, the areas where street crime is rampant have tremendous potential for economic growth because of easy access to rail lines, highways, electric power, and a large supply of available labor. Many of these areas were rich in the past.

Crime takes a terrible toll on communities in terms of loss of human and fiscal capital. Criminals steal and destroy property, drive away customers and investors, reduce property values, and depreciate a neighborhood's quality of life. Businesses close and working families move away. Stewart says that crime "is the ultimate tax on enterprise ... when the marketplace cannot assert itself when the local economy is regulated by crime."[10]

As far as individual criminal behavior, people of all socioeconomic levels commit crimes. Although there may be some truth to the fact that more poor people are in prison because the rich can afford better lawyers, in many of our prisons, especially in the federal system, one is apt to find several upper-middle-class, white-collar criminals.

Early in my career at the US penitentiary McNeil Island, I was in charge of the inmate reference and law libraries. I had an inmate crew that worked for me. They mostly consisted of former professionals, such as lawyers, engineers, and CPAs. They were all white, educated, and doing well financially but had decided they wanted to rob banks, sell drugs, or swindle people out of money. I also had a few guys who were former street thugs. None of them matched the profile of the poverty-stricken, uneducated minorities that supposedly overpopulated our prisons.

In 1976, Samuel Yochelson and Stanton Samenow published a groundbreaking book in criminal psychology, *The Criminal Personality*. For eight years, the two of them studied both jailed criminals and the criminally insane at Saint Elizabeth's Hospital, Washington DC. Like most criminal psychologists, they began their work believing that crooks were the maladjusted products of bad environments. But after probing the psyches of hundreds of inmates, they decided that the criminals weren't sick, they were just very good at manipulating psychologists. Convinced that classic psychology was wasted on these men, they devised a therapeutic technique designed to force criminals to confront their behavior realistically.[11]

Certain people have a criminal personality. They commit crimes "not for the need but for the greed," as inmates used to tell me. Rehabilitation as we understand it, such as merely providing education, drug treatment, and job training, will only produce educated, drug-free criminals with job skills. In order to change these types of offenders, the work must focus on their criminal psyche, but even then, there's no assurances of change.

I myself know that people can reform themselves because I've seen it happen. This, however, is a matter of personal responsibility. The most the system can do is provide opportunities for change and point people in the right direction.

Whenever we hear that poverty causes crime, we must ask, "Why don't the vast majority of poor people commit crime? Aren't there any people in prison who are educated and come from financially well-off families? If so, how do you rehabilitate them?"

Myth #2: Prisons are filled with low-level, nonviolent offenders.

First of all, the percentage of violent offenders in state prisons increased during a recent twenty-year period.

In 1991, 45 percent of all state prisoners—or an estimated 327,000 offenders—were sentenced to more than one year for violent offenses. On December 31, 2006 (the year in which admissions to state prisons reached their peak), 50 percent of all sentenced prisoners in custody of state correctional authorities were violent offenders.

In 2011, more than 53 percent (or an estimated 718,000 offenders) of the year-end population was serving a sentence for a violent crime. While robbery was the most common offense across the twenty-year period, the proportion of violent offenders convicted for murder or any sexual assault increased over time.[12]

Justice reformers shout loudly about our prisons being filled with non-violent offenders. This raises several questions. Should we only incarcerate violent offenders? What about car thieves, burglars, drug dealers, swindlers, and others? Should we never incarcerate these types of criminals? What exactly is a nonviolent offender? Is it someone who has never committed a violent crime? Is it someone convicted of a nonviolent crime but with a history of violence? Is it someone who committed a violent crime but was convicted of a nonviolent crime through plea bargaining? The point is that sentencing statistics provide only a snapshot of the person's current offense. They tell nothing about a person's prior criminal history or circumstances of the crime.

We should remember that Al Capone was convicted and served time for tax evasion. Based solely on this, he would have been considered a nonviolent offender. We, of course, know the real story. The federal prison system has always had an abundance of other such "nonviolent offenders."

When I was a case manager at the US penitentiary Lewisburg, I had a particular inmate in my caseload serving time for interstate transportation of stolen property. The actual crime consisted of him and an accomplice breaking into a home in a well-to-do part of Boston and robbing the residents (an elderly couple) at gunpoint. They forced the man to give up the combination to the house safe by pistol-whipping his wife. They fled Boston across the state line to New Hampshire, with the police on their tail (a neighbor hearing the victims' screams had called the police, who arrived as the robbers were making their getaway).

They were finally stopped and arrested, but not before a firefight that resulted in a wounded cop. The states of New Hampshire and Massachusetts filed charges against the pair for assault with a firearm on a police officer and armed robbery. They picked up the federal charge of interstate transportation of stolen property because of their flight across state lines—same crime but different charges. One charge suggests a nonviolent crime and nonviolent offenders. The other charges don't. Both robbers also had extensive prior criminal records, including violent offenses.

The robber who was in my caseload was denied federal parole much to his dismay. He claimed to be a "non-violent offender" based on his crime of conviction. The parole commission disagreed and made their decision on what they termed "total offence behavior."

People usually don't end up in prison based on a single offense but on a combination of prior criminal and personal histories and the true nature of the crime itself rather than what may have been the final charge at sentencing with or without plea-bargaining.

An important consideration from the victims' perspective, regardless of the violent or nonviolent nature of crime, is often ignored. Many experts may consider nonviolent crimes, such as burglary, as petty or low-level, but the public and especially victims disagree. What the public seems to understand but experts don't is that it's not just a matter of the value or amount stolen that makes a crime petty or serious. It's the breach of the victim's privacy and security that makes him or her feel personally violated and vulnerable.

Whenever someone says that prisons are filled with nonviolent, low-level offenders, we should ask, "What exactly is a nonviolent offender? What exactly is a low-level offender?" Just as a person's college major alone tells nothing about the person's academic record, such as GPA and courses studied, a person's current crime of conviction tells nothing about a person's criminal history and details of the offense.

Myth #3: Prisons are filled with people arrested for simple possession of drugs.

David Boaz, executive vice president of the libertarian CATO Institute once stated:

> I probably didn't help my case by noting that our last three presidents have acknowledged using illegal drugs, and it is

just incomprehensible to me how they can morally justify arresting other people for doing the same thing they did. Do they think that they would have been better off if they had been arrested and incarcerated for their youthful drug use? Do they think the country would have been better off if they had been arrested and incarcerated? If not, how do they justify punishing others?[13]

Longer sentences for narcotics distribution and other drug-related offenses are indeed one reason for increasing prison populations. This, however, promotes the myth that, because of the war on drugs, our prisons are filled with drug users arrested for simple possession and use of drugs, including marijuana. This leaves the impression of countless of individuals sitting at home, minding their own business, smoking a joint or doing a line of coke, when the SWAT team kicked down their door and hauled them off to prison.

There is not one police department in the country that has the resources or inclination to engage in such time-consuming and wasteful tactics. The fact is that most arrests for simple possession of marijuana or other drugs occur during the course of investigations for other criminal activities.

For example, the police may receive a BOLO (be on the look out) for an armed robbery suspect. They see a person matching the suspect's description and pull him over. During a pat down, the police find some drugs in his possession. If the person is not the suspect they were looking for, chances are he'll receive probation for the possession charge. If he is, he'll be faced with charges of armed robbery plus possession.

If the person is the suspect they were looking for and has an extensive criminal record, but the witness is intimidated into not pressing charges, the police might take what they can get and have the defendant charged, convicted, and jailed for simple drug possession. Remember what happened to Al Capone?

It's safe to say that there are not many individuals doing hard time in our prison system for simple possession of a few joints of marijuana or small amounts of drugs. Most people serving time for drug possession are those who are in possession of drugs in order to distribute them and/or are part of an organized network of drug distribution. These are the types of cases the police and justice system are concerned with and thus spend the vast amount of time and resources pursuing.

As far as the connection between drug use and crime, there is indication that drug-addicted individuals tend to commit more crime as their drug use increases. Most important, research indicates that most heroin-addicted criminals were involved in crime before they became addicted.[14] This applies to those using other drugs. The criminal behavior preceded the beginning of drug use.

When we hear that prisons are filled or have high volumes of individuals for simple possession of drugs and drug use, we should ask, "How so?" There are probably tens of millions of Americans who use drugs recreationally. If we were to try to arrest and imprison half or even one quarter of them, wouldn't our police become exhausted and police departments bankrupted? Wouldn't the entire criminal justice system collapse under such weight? We could never begin to have enough prison capacity to house everyone.

Myth #4: Prisons are overcrowded, harsh, and violent human warehouses and schools of crime.

In order to call attention to the urgency of the criminal justice problem, a "corrections crisis" has been declared. It states that our nation's prisons are dangerously overcrowded and enormously expensive. They pose a hazard to the lives of inmates and staff as well as to the fiscal stability of states.

The problem with this scenario is that it is misleading at best and fictitious at worst. The problem with prison overcrowding has less to do with increasing inmate populations than with shifting definitions of overcrowding based on the following designations:

Design capacity: the number of inmates that planners or architects intended for the facility

Operational capacity: the number of inmates that can be accommodated based on a facility's staff, existing programs, and services

Rated capacity: the number of beds or inmates assigned by a rating official to institutions within the jurisdiction

Based on these three different standards, no one knew (or knows) the level of prison overcrowding. Prison overcrowding is a fluid concept that's been used as a political football by all sides of the corrections debate in order to push a certain agenda. Most importantly, prison crowding ignores the real issues of inmate and staff safety and security as well as institutional manageability—which have all greatly improved in the past twenty years.

Experts have long predicted that our overcrowded prisons would soon erupt into violence in a rash of disturbances. In fact, just the opposite has happened. Prisons have become much more peaceful in the past thirty years. Better staff training and inmate classification systems have dramatically decreased prison homicides.

The Bureau of Justice Statistics manages the Deaths in Custody Reporting Program (DCRP). Records show that between 1980 and 2002, the state prison homicide rate dropped from 54.0 per 100,000 inmates to an astounding 5.7 per 100,000. Better architectural design of facilities has also made Attica-type uprisings virtually a thing of the past.

Between 1983 and 2002, jail suicide rates dropped 64 percent. State prison suicide rates, historically much lower than the rate in jails, dropped from 34 per 100,000 inmates to 14 per 100,000 during the same period.

Deaths from all causes, including homicide, suicide, illness, intoxication, and accidental injury, declined from 3,414 in 2009 to 3,232 in 2010, for a total decrease of 5 percent, which is the largest decline in the number of prison deaths since the DCRP began collecting prisoner mortality data in 2001.[15]

Courts and legislatures call for nonviolent inmates or defendants to be released or not incarcerated because of prison overcrowding, yet no one bothers to ask the critical questions that must be asked. What exactly is a nonviolent offender? What constitutes prison overcrowding? What is our primary and ultimate goal—to reduce the prison population or to create and maintain safer communities?

That's the reason why every instance of sentencing or court-imposed reform results in calls for more reform. Prison populations continue expanding or aren't greatly reduced. Imagine the confusion if hospitals were ordered to reduce their percentages of people who were not "seriously ill" or had an illness that was "not potentially life threatening" and could be treated by other means. In the first place, doctors don't refer the vast majority of their patients to the hospitals. More specifically, the terms "not seriously ill" and "not potentially life threatening" are open to interpretation. Influenza can be potentially life threatening to an eighty-year-old but not necessarily to a twenty-year-old.

Most important, attempts to send fewer people to hospitals wouldn't change the fact that as a matter of course the vast majority of people don't end up as hospital patients after getting sick. It's just as important to know that the vast majority of people don't end up as prison inmates after a criminal conviction.

As for prisons being nothing but human warehouses and schools of crime, in the BOP and in state prisons, an inmate can enter as a functional illiterate and leave with a college degree. He/she can receive job training in various vocational trades, such as computers. He/she has access to counselors, caseworkers, psychologists, and other professionals. Some inmates choose not to take advantage of any opportunities for self-improvement. These tend to be the ones who are released, commit another crime, and, when arrested, declare that "they didn't rehabilitate me" or all they learned in prison was how to be a better criminal.

This view of prisons being only schools of crime ignores the fact that many inmates were raised in poor, crime-infested neighborhoods where they learned their criminality, and they'll return to these neighborhoods and environments upon release. When most people enter prison, they're already journeymen in the criminal trade.

Whenever we hear that prisons are too overcrowded, and that we should stop or cut down on incarceration, we should ask, "Should we stop or cut down on hospitalization because hospitals are too crowded?" If prisons are only schools of crime, what did offenders learn in their crime-infested neighborhoods before they were arrested, and what will they learn in those same neighborhoods upon release? Just as people who are raised in bad neighborhoods can learn to be responsible individuals, can't people in prison also learn other things besides crime?"

Myth #5: Prisons are too expensive and take money from vital services, such as education.

Americans tend to be fiscally conservative, so it's important to spin the corrections narrative to suggest that it's too expensive, drains resources from other vital areas, and threatens to bankrupt the states.

We're spending too much on prisons at the expense of vital programs, such as education for our children. Our nation now has the shameful distinction of having the world's highest incarceration rate.

The news media, ever mindful of conveying crisis information, consistently print stories of how terribly expensive prisons are to the taxpayer. These are some headlines from 2005 alone:

PRISON COSTS ARE RUNNING OUT OF CONTROL (*Denver Post*)[16]

REPORT: PRISON COSTS HURTING EDUCATION
(*Charleston Gazette*, West Virginia)[17]

PRISONS EAT UP TAX DOLLARS (*Wisconsin State Journal*, Madison)[18]

As with all other issues in the reform narrative, the language doesn't square with the facts. According to the Bureau of Justice Statistics, since 2003, corrections expenditures, as a share of total spending, fluctuated between 2.5 percent and 2.9 percent of state expenditures.

Between 1982 and 2010, spending on education varied between 29 percent and 33 percent of total state expenditures, spending on public welfare varied between 22 percent and 25 percent, spending on highways varied between 5.7 percent and 8.6 percent, and spending on health care and hospitals varied between 6.2 percent and 7.5 percent. Other expenditures (including air transportation, financial administration, police protection, and public safety expenditures) ranged between 29 percent and 32 percent of state expenditures.

In 2010, states spent $48.5 billion on corrections. By comparison, states spent $571.3 billion on education and $462.7 billion on public welfare.[19]

The reality is that, contrary to what we hear about states spending money on prisons at the expense of education and other vital services, spending on prisons is far less than we're led to believe. Not only is spending on prisons not hurting education, states spend more than ten times on education than on corrections. It should also be noted that prisons make up only one portion (albeit the largest) of total spending on corrections. Total spending includes probation, parole, and other community corrections programs. That's in accordance with how a free society like ours should prioritize its spending.

In these times of colossal government spending and fiscal irresponsibility, we *should* worry about our country's financial security. But compared to other line items, what we spend on corrections is peanuts.

One thing to remember is that attempts to save money by putting fewer people in prison are often ill conceived and therefore don't produce the intended results. In 2014 Indiana overhauled its criminal code in order to allow violent offenders to serve more time in state prisons while those convicted of less serious felonies serve their sentences in local jails or local corrections programs.

Apparently, no one bothered to consider that Indiana already had 83 percent of its corrections population under community supervision rather than locked up. Local sheriffs complained that leaving more inmates in county jails would merely shift costs to the counties. Furthermore, putting more people into community corrections would require hiring more probation officers and case managers. This brilliant act of reform will no doubt require more reform measures in the future.[20]

Whenever we hear that we spend too much on prisons we should ask, "Too much relative to what?"

Myth #6: Our criminal justice system is racist. Prisons hold a disproportionate amount of blacks and minorities.

Most Americans believe that people are arrested and convicted because they violated and harmed a victim's life, liberty, or property. Most criminal justice reformers don't seem to hold this view. To them, our country is an oppressive and racist society that targets minorities in general but blacks particular.

America is also supposed to be a sexist society even though women constitute about 51 percent of the population. Males make up about 90 percent of the prison population. That's why you hardly (if at all) hear criticism of our justice system based on the latter because the former seems so obvious.

Evidence produced by several studies as well as statistics paint a different picture. Blacks are overrepresented in incarceration rates, but that's because of the black crime rate. According to the Bureau of Justice Statistics:

Blacks are disproportionately represented as both homicide victims and offenders. The victimization rate for blacks in 2008 (27.8 per 100,000) was six times higher than the rate for whites (4.5 per 100,000). Blacks committed crimes at a rate (34.4 per 100,000) that was almost eight times higher than the rate for whites (4.5 per 100,000).[21]

In 1980, the black forcible-rape arrest rate was seven times greater than the white arrest rate. This changed between1980 to 2009, when the black forcible-rape arrest rate declined 70 percent. In contrast, between 1980 and 2009, the white arrest rate for forcible rape declined 31 percent.[22]

Between 1980 and 2009, an average of 40 percent of all arrests for robbery were white arrests, 59 percent were black arrests. On average, the black arrest rate for robbery was ten times the white rate. The black arrest rate for burglary was three times the white arrest rate. These arrests are based not only on what the police reported but also on the eyewitness testimony of the victims, most of whom were black. It bears repeating that blacks make up the majority of victims, which means that most black crime is black-on-black crime.[23]

Black criminals who live in several major cities are often arrested by black police officers working for black chiefs of police in cities that have black mayors. In these cities, blacks make up a good portion of the area's criminal justice professionals, including judges and prosecutors. Black criminals are also likely to be found guilty by juries with a large representation of black and minority members.

This does not mean we shouldn't be troubled by the existence of racism in our society. What should trouble all of us is the sense of misplaced compassion of so many experts who advocate for the people who prey on the lives and properties of the very poor minority residents who live in the inner city because they can't afford to live anywhere else. Most of these experts don't live in poor, inner-city, crime-plagued areas but in white middle- and upper-middle-class communities. It's easy to advocate for street thugs when they don't surround your own home.

Whenever we hear that the criminal justice system incarcerates too may blacks and minorities, we should ask, "Too many regarding their numbers in the system, or too many regarding the crimes they commit?"

Myth #7: The United States has the most punitive criminal justice system in the world.

This is based on our incarceration rates, which are supposedly the highest in the world. I say supposedly because many countries maintain terrible records, and they use punishments other than prison, such as making certain "undesirables" simply disappear. If we have the world's highest incarceration rate, that means our rates are higher than countries like North Korea, Iran, Cuba, and others. Does this mean that we should try to be more like those countries?

This myth was born when the National Council on Crime and Delinquency (NCCD) announced to the media that, in terms of prisoners per capita, only two countries (the Soviet Union and South Africa) were more ruthlessly repressive than the United States. The media ate this up and has been promoting the myth ever since. They never bothered to ask the NCCD why they were so willing to accept Soviet figures at face value or why the Soviets neglected to include the four or five million prisoners in their forced labor camps.[24]

A December 30, 2013, story by the Associated Press indicated that the Greek prison system was on the brink of collapse. More than thirty men were crammed into one cell, locked up night and day for weeks or months. Without enough bunks, many slept on the floor. The windows were painted over, blocking out the sun, and the air was thick with cigarette smoke and the reek from the one toilet everyone shared. Hundreds of inmates are caged for months as they await trial in police holding cells designed for stints of hours or, at most, days.[25]

According to records, Greece has an incarceration rate of 120 per 100,000 people compared to the United States with an incarceration rate of 707 per 100,000.[26] What good is having a low incarceration rate if your prisons are hellholes of squalor and your system is collapsing? This shows that incarceration rates are, for all practical purposes, meaningless.

Whenever we hear that the United States has the highest incarceration rate in the world, there are so many questions we should ask, such as: So what? Does this mean we're more repressive than countries like North Korea, Iran, and others? If yes, how so? How do we know? Can we trust other countries' data? If our prisons are safer, and provide more healthy environments than the prisons in countries with low incarceration rates, isn't this more important than where we rank?

The most important questions with regard to incarceration in general are: How much incarceration is too much and why? Is there a "magic number"? If yes, what is it? How is it determined and why? Should we stop sending people to prison after we reach that number?

Recognizing these myths is crucial to understanding the true nature of the problem and thus crafting practical policy with beneficial solutions. If we fail to ask the questions we just explored, it may lead to terrible and unintended consequences.

As a result of an inmate lawsuit in California in 2001, the state had to spend billions of dollars in new medical facilities and staff plus reduce its inmate population to 110,000. California transferred thousands of inmates to county jails, thereby increasing the jail population. Several other inmates were transferred out of state to private prisons, but the courts blocked the state from increasing these transfers. California argued that the state would have to release serious and violent offenders.

The state also argued that it lacked lower-risk offenders who could safely be released early because most of those were already being sentenced to county jails instead of state prisons. More importantly California, as is the case nationally, already had and has the vast majority of its corrections population under community supervision rather than locked up. On February 10, 2014, the courts granted California a two-year extension on its deadline to reduce the inmate population. California had planned to spend seventy million dollars to house inmates in private, out-of-state facilities. Because the court blocked any further out of state transfers, the state opted to spend eighty-one million dollars for the rehabilitation programs intended to reduce the recidivism rate and help bring the prison population down over time."[27]

Apparently, the court believed that the state complying with its order to reduce prison overcrowding by transferring prisoners to other states was a bad idea.

In the world of academia, defense attorneys, and other assorted experts, rehabilitation seems to consist of a magic pill or sets of treatments that can be administered to offenders and thus transform criminals into responsible, law-abiding citizens. Corrections apparently fails to provide these magic pills or treatments either because of incompetence or a preference for harsh punishment. Many people are now satisfied that spending eighty-one million dollars rather than seventy million dollars is a better "investment" because the money will now be spent on rehabilitation and thus reduce recidivism and prison crowding. The system will supposedly be able to buy more "magic pills" and administer them to the inmates, thereby preventing most of them from returning. The state will thus save a ton of money and all will be well.

One can imagine the not-too-distant future when cries for more reform resume because of continued prison crowding. It's easy to imagine that the charges will be brought upon by the state. Eighty-one million dollars was not enough or was directed at the "wrong" programs. More money must be spent to fix a "system that's too expensive." Meanwhile, California sinks deeper into financial ruin.

The prescribed solutions to what ails the criminal justice system often do little or nothing to solve the problem. That's because offender advocates are considered criminal justice experts. Experts provide policymakers with answers rather than help them ask the right questions. The answers are based on myths about the system, which have become established within the criminal justice reform movement.

The criminal justice reform narrative is essentially anti-incarceration, and strives for less imprisonment without a systemic view or approach to the problem. Reform advocates are essentially offender advocates that consider prisons and imprisonment cruel and harsh measures unfit for a democratic society except for the most violent offenders.

The unintended consequences of this authoritative strategy ensure that reforms are constantly called for because the real problems are never solved. This begs the question if, in fact, these consequences are actually unintended.

CHAPTER 3

Taking the "Order" out of Law and Order

In the Zen tradition, the master carries a "keisaku" (a long, flat stick) as he walks among the meditating monks. After sitting in the lotus position for several minutes, one loses concentration and the pain to the legs can become excruciating. When the master or teacher walks in front of a meditator who's at the limit of endurance, he bows and remains, with his back exposed. This is to request that the master strike him several blows to the back and shoulders with the flat end of the keisaku. It's not considered to be punitive but rather is a compassionate means to reinvigorate and awaken the meditators and thus assist them on their path to enlightenment.

As a young correctional officer at McNeil Island, Washington, in the 1970s, a staff psychologist and myself formed a Zen meditation group for inmates. We had the fortune of securing a visit from a Japanese Zen monk who was visiting the area. He participated in a meditation session with us and used the keisaku freely. After the session, one inmate told me that if his parents had ever struck him with such love and compassion, he might never have ended up in prison. To be clear, this is not an endorsement of child abuse or any other harsh, destructive methods. This is to illustrate how discipline and order became negative terms in our society.

The second half of the twentieth century produced tremendous change in our country. Our triumph over militaristic tyranny in World War ll had propelled the United States into a dominant world power and into a cold war with another tyrannical power, communism. Apparently, many people found it increasingly difficult to justify having institutions that suppress freedom in the land of the free.

During the final decades of the twentieth century, public policy drifted

31

away from enforcing control and public order to maximizing individual liberty. The mentally ill were deinstitutionalized, public drunkenness was decriminalized, and begging and public solicitation became more tolerated. Many of these policies were the result of court actions rather than because of public demands.

In 1973, the US District Court for the District of Columbia ruled in Souder v Brennan that patients in mental health institutions must be considered employees and paid a minimum wage whenever they performed any work within the institution. Although our country had been progressing toward deinstitutionalizing the mentally ill for at least two decades, this ruling hastened the effort. States could no longer afford to house patients that had to be paid for their work, which led to the closing of several state hospitals.[28]

During this time period, Social Security Supplemental Security Income (SSI) became available to people with disabilities. Beginning in the 1950s, new drugs were developed that reduced severe psychotic symptoms, which allowed the mentally ill to function in less-structured environments.

Community mental-health services were often uncoordinated and unable to meet complex needs. Existing patients were discharged only to become homeless or end up in jail, and jails became the new mental-health institutions. The law of unintended consequences is one law that reformers continuously seem to ignore. This is especially true with current justice-reform efforts.

Our courts, as our justice system in general, were designed to process individual cases. Courts process cases brought on behalf of individual beggars, public drunkards, or loiterers. These individuals seldom represent a physical threat to anyone, and so the threat to public order is ignored in the process. This means that courts tend to rule in favor of the defendant.

As many individuals take advantage of the rights granted to one individual, public order and maintenance begins to break down. More cases of individual beggars, drunks, and loiterers begin to clog up the courts, which results in less enforcement of these types of offenses. As the public complains to the police about deteriorating conditions in their neighborhoods, they seem powerless to intervene. The job of the police, after all, is to apprehend serious criminals, and arresting these types of individuals is thus considered a waste of time. Besides, if they were to actually arrest a beggar or vagrant, the case would be dismissed in court, as the courts also have more important cases to attend to and process.

Many advocates for the poor and homeless began to advocate success-fully for the abolishment of vagrancy and loitering laws. In response, many cities and jurisdictions began replacing these "status" laws (laws directed at a person's status, such as homelessness) with laws directed at specific behaviors (loitering "for the purpose of"). These laws focused on specific behaviors were directed at combating disorder rather than attacking an individual's status. This is an important distinction that advocates and many courts failed or refused to see.[29]

This philosophy of decriminalization and deinstitutionalization spread among various aspects of public policy. In 1967, President Johnson's Commission on Law Enforcement condemned the treatment of individuals arrested for public drunkenness. Persons arrested for drunkenness were held in stark "drunk tanks" and released when they sobered up without regard for the underlying problem of alcoholism. Reformers in the 1950s and 1960s became justifiably concerned about the lack of treatment and redefined the problem from that of a crime to that of an illness. At the same time, however, they recognized that the vast majority of chronic drunks would never seek treatment on their own.

The proposed solution was involuntary commitment for alcoholics, but this angered civil libertarians who saw this as an infringement on per-sonal liberty. In response, civil libertarians managed to transform institu-tional commitment for alcoholism from a medical issue into a legal issue. President Johnson's crime commission endorsed the decriminalization of drunkenness. Consequently, drunkenness would no longer result in arrest or commitment unless it was accompanied by other criminal behavior.

Decriminalization of drunkenness and the deinstitutionalization of the mentally ill was a big blow for destabilization of public order in our cities. Adequate numbers of community mental-health and detox centers were never built for a variety of reasons. The mentally ill and alcoholics asserted a right to their lifestyles and refused any assistance. As the sheer numbers of mentally ill and drunk people on the streets increased, the police became overwhelmed and powerless to reduce the growing disorder.

As I discussed in the previous chapter, public disorder creates the conditions for crime to flourish. Deteriorating conditions and crime cause many of the working families to flee to other more promising locations. Businesses begin to lose customers and also abandon the neighborhood or community. This exodus of people and businesses deprives the general community of jobs and a stable tax base, thereby creating a more impoverished community. In short, crime causes poverty rather than the other way around.

In an article of the March 1982 edition of *The Atlantic Monthly*, social scientists James Q. Wilson and George L. Kelling described the snowball effect of deteriorating urban environmental conditions caused by crime and disorder. They wrote:

> Consider a building with a few broken windows. If the windows are not repaired, the tendency is for vandals to break a few more windows. Eventually, they may even break into the building, and if it's unoccupied, perhaps become squatters or light fires inside.
>
> Or consider a pavement. Some litter accumulates. Soon, more litter accumulates. Eventually, people even start leaving bags of refuse from take-out restaurants there or even break into cars.[30]

This became known as the Broken Windows Theory, which became and remains controversial within criminology. Traditional criminologists tend to view crime in terms of individual criminal behavior, and the social forces and factors that affect a particular individual, or individuals, to commit crime. The Broken Windows Theory defines, or, more specifically, separates, crime from individual criminal behavior. To be sure, both criminal behavior and crime should be addressed in public safety policy. But it's most important to place the individual behavior within the overall context of the general conditions within neighborhoods and communities in order to address the problem of crime. If we want to reduce crime, we should focus on crime and the ways to confront it rather than react to individual criminal behavior after the fact. By focusing on the central issue, we can do a better job of addressing all other related problems.

Many progressive intellectual elites refused to see deteriorating social order in a negative light. Many proclaimed graffiti as a new urban art form. They spoke out against "harassment" of the homeless by the police. The homeless became the latest cause to rally around. Individuals and agencies visited the homeless at night, delivering fast food meals and blankets. Morning would find the visited sites filled with garbage heaps of discarded fast-food containers and blankets. Neighborhoods sank deeper into disorder, and its residents sank deeper into despair.

One of the most devastating results of deteriorating public order was the crack epidemic of the 1980s. Crack dealers, as well as other drug dealers, began to openly sell their products in "open air" drug markets. Citizens who had to walk by these drug markets and assorted menacing individuals who frequented them became more frightened. As the inevitable violence that's part of the illegal drug industry flared up, more working families fled to other communities considered safer while those who had no choice but to remain became hostages to their surroundings.

Those who had no choice but to remain were mostly poor and minorities. The crack epidemic had devastating consequences on the black community, so much so that black community leaders petitioned their representatives in congress to intervene. Contrary to popular current belief about the disparities in sentencing for crack versus powder cocaine being racist because more blacks than whites use and sell crack, Heather McDonald sets the record straight:

> The assertion that concern about crack resulted from "unconscious racial aversion towards blacks" ignores a key fact: black leaders were the first to sound the alarm about the drug, as Harvard law professor Randall Kennedy documents in Race, Crime, and the Law. Harlem congressman Charles Rangel initiated the federal response to the epidemic, warning the House of Representatives in March 1986 that crack had made cocaine "frightening[ly]" accessible to youth. A few months later, Brooklyn congressman Major Owens explicitly rejected what is now received wisdom about media hype. "None of the press accounts really have exaggerated what is actually going on," Owens said; the crack epidemic was "as bad as any articles have stated." Queens congressman Alton Waldon then called on his colleagues to act: "For those of us who are black this self-inflicted pain is the worst oppression we have known since slavery. ... Let us ... pledge to crack down on crack." The bill that eventually passed, containing the crack/powder distinction, won majority support among black congressmen, none of whom, as Kennedy points out, objected to it as racist.[31]

I think it's fair to say that any white congressman who had refused to support the legislation would have been labeled a racist or uncaring about the plight of the black community.

Accounts filled the daily news about individuals receiving two wildly unequal sentences for the same crime but sentenced by different judges. More people began to enter the correctional system as inmates but primarily on probation or parole. The relatively lax supervision of traditional community corrections resulted in many offenders on probation and parole victimizing the public and thus being revoked and incarcerated.

As citizens became more fearful, they also became fed up with a criminal justice system that didn't seem to represent their interests. Crime victims felt especially neglected and resented the fact that those who harmed them were the main focus of concern of those working in the system while they were left to fend for themselves. After victims performed their roles as witnesses for the prosecution, they were forgotten. The charges were brought by the state and for the state against individual offenders with little or no regard for the well-being and safety of the entire community.

As politicians, eager to hold onto their positions, caught wind of citizens' anger, they responded in the only way they knew how: they passed more and tougher laws. The indeterminate sentencing that had dominated the earlier part of the century turned into mandatory minimums and sentencing guidelines. Indeterminate sentencing had provided judges with more discretion and options and did not specify a definite period of confinement (i.e., five to ten years rather than ten years or five years). It also resulted in wildly different sentences for various offenders for the same type of crime. The public deemed this unfair, plus the fact that some might be released a lot sooner than anticipated. As the public saw it, inmates were being released much too soon on parole only to continue victimizing the public.

The result was "mandatory minimums," which dictated a mandatory minimum sentence that must be served for a particular crime, and sentencing guidelines, which stipulated sentences within a certain range of guidelines (i.e., no less than a sentence of between eight to ten years) and even the abolition of parole in some states. All this seemed to do little to placate public alienation from the justice system.

To the justice reform movement, it seemed that this was a step back from what had been a steady distancing from more incarceration. Instead, it seemed that we were participating in a mass incarceration of our citizens, or at least that's the impression they wanted to imprint. Prison should hold nothing but the most violent offenders and all others should be in "alternatives."

Many in academia and in high levels of the criminal justice establishment believed that the more punitive sentencing laws violated this basic tenet of imprisonment. According to them, our nation was on an incarceration binge with large numbers of low-level, nonviolent offenders being locked up along with thousands of people guilty of nothing more than using and abusing drugs. An all-out effort should therefore be mounted to reverse this senseless trend.

The focus of the work would be on the policymakers in Washington DC, and in state capitals. Papers and articles were written decrying our nations "obsession" with incarceration. Well-established justice- reform, special-interest groups lobbied politicians. NIC and other national training and consulting groups began instructing jurisdictions on diverting people away from prison. More programs to better monitor people under community supervision, such as home confinement with electronic monitoring and intensive supervision programs, were promoted.

These "intermediate sanctions/punishments" programs were valuable and desirable innovations, but they were promoted for the wrong reason and were marketed with dishonest or misleading methods. They were promoted as prison diversion programs, but since the overall majority of offenders were and are already under community supervision, few people were diverted.

Being ever mindful that the public was hell-bent on punishment, a type of reverse psychology was called for. The pitch was made that these programs were a smarter way of punishment and a smart way of being tough on crime. Would presenting a "smarter" option presuppose that the person being presented to was dumb or had pursued a not-too-smart path? Why worry about such questions when, as an expert, you have the answers?

Many of these reformers boasted of their marketing prowess. In conversations, I'd often hear them explain that they could market these programs to anyone, whether liberal or conservative. If speaking to liberals, they'd use the traditional narrative of presenting these programs as a kinder alternative to the cruelty and harshness of prisons. If speaking to conservatives, they'd reverse the thought process and present these programs as tougher than imprisonment. Prisoners, after all, did nothing but sit in their cell or lift weights and watch TV. In these alternative programs, they had to work, have frequent drug tests, and support themselves and their families. The problem was that this fit the false narrative held among many in the general population that our nation's prisons and jails are too cushy and soft and should be more severe. It may have had some unintended consequences.

In 1993, Joe Arpaio was elected sheriff of Maricopa County, Arizona. Much to the delight of his constituents and displeasure of prison reformers, he instituted more stringent conditions at the jail. These included setting up tents for living quarters in the hot sun, making the inmates wear pink jump suits, and serving baloney sandwiches for meals. He seemed to delight in the national notoriety he gained, which infuriated offender advocates to no end. But ... could it be that Sheriff Joe Arpaio became a success because of the criminal justice reform movement? We can only contemplate the irony.

Intermediate sanctions programs were also sold as being cheaper and more cost effective than prison, so the overall costs of corrections would be cut. Because of the fact that most people are under community supervision, the vast majority of offenders would be drawn from those who'd normally end up on probation rather than diverting them away from prison. This alone defeated the stated purpose of these programs. As far as the cost factor, the vast majority of people are on probation, which costs practically nothing compared to prison. Putting more people into these more intensive supervision programs with drug treatment and greater surveillance would actually *increase* rather than decrease costs.

A better rationale would be to point out the fact that most offenders are on probation and receive very little to no supervision. More importantly, they're out in the community where they interact directly with the public. It would therefore be more *valuable,* but more costly, to have tighter control, supervision, and treatment options for these individuals.

As far as costs, no one knows the exact cost of imprisonment, but estimates run from a low of forty billion dollars to a high of eighty billion dollars in federal, state, and local tax dollars per year. This compares to about one trillion dollars the federal government spends on entitlements, such as social security benefits, plus hundreds of billions for other individual line items, including education. Even the high estimate of eighty billion dollars per year is peanuts in comparison.

The reform movement of the 1980s and 1990s resulted in most states implementing intermediate sanctions programs. This didn't result in a tremendous reduction in incarceration. Instead of asking why and examining the functions of entire system, the calls for more of these programs became louder.

Prison populations *did* increase sharply in the 1980s and 1990s, but it wasn't primarily or entirely because of more punitive laws and longer sentences. In 1991, Patrick A. Langan from the Bureau of Justice Statistics published an article in *Science* that shattered some myths about the cause of rising prison populations. He determined that the growth was due to increase in prison admissions rather than to longer sentences or time served.[32] Prosecutors convicted more felons, judges imposed more prison sentences, and more probation and parole violators were sent or returned to prison. The system had become more efficient but not harsher.

The greater use of technology had a huge impact on the system's improved efficiency. Police and other criminal justice departments around the country became interconnected through new computer technologies. Two technologies in particular, the Automated Fingerprint Identification System (AFIS) and DNA testing were truly revolutionary in crime solving.

Prior to AFIS, the process of comparing and matching fingerprints was very time consuming and labor intensive. Police departments had to compare and match prints lifted from crime scenes with millions of fingerprints on file in their own departments or at the FBI in Washington DC. Most often, the best way to get a match was to arrest a suspect, take his prints, and match them to the ones lifted at the crime scene. AFIS allowed police to enter fingerprints lifted at crime scenes into the automated system. The system would then electronically compare the lifted prints from a database of thousands of prints on file.

The FBI had been working on automating the system since the 1960s, but it wasn't until the 1980s and 1990s that the technologies advanced enough to create an integrated and interconnected system. In 1999, the FBI created a centralized, automated national fingerprint system called the Integrated Automated Fingerprint Identification System (IAFIS). This connects state and local AFIS information systems and technologies to a central location containing more than one hundred million prints. The process of matching fingerprints went from a process that could take weeks or months to one that takes minutes or hours.

DNA testing was still in relative obscurity when it was highly publicized during the O.J. Simpson murder trial of 1995. The science for the testing had been advancing since the 1980s, and at the same time, courts had decided the admissibility of DNA results in criminal trials. After legal victories for DNA admissibility, the FBI created the Combined DNA Index System (CODIS) forensic DNA database, mandated by the federal DNA Identification Act of 1994. Today, in addition to CODIS, all fifty states maintain DNA databases as a result of legislation.

DNA database legislation has given rise to a new type of arrest warrant—termed "John Doe" or "DNA" warrants—because the warrant is issued not for a named person but for a genetic code identified as part of a criminal investigation for which no suspect has been identified and no database match has yet been found.

In September 1999, a district attorney in Wisconsin became one of the first prosecutors to obtain a warrant and file criminal charges against a man identified in the warrant solely by his DNA profile. The primary purpose of these warrants is to extend the statute of limitations in cases of violent crimes. Many states have successfully convicted offenders based on John Doe warrants, and several, such as Wisconsin, have passed legislation legalizing their use.[33]

Meanwhile, as reformers and politicians wrung their hands regarding how to stop mass incarceration, our cities descended into greater disorder and citizens became more fearful of street crime. It would take fed-up citizens who had had enough of living in fear to awaken the system into doing something to address the problems of our neighborhoods and communities. The police were the first to heed the call.

CHAPTER 4

Community Policing: Back to the Future

> The police at all times should maintain a relationship with the public that gives reality to the historic tradition that the police are the public and that the public are the police; the police are the only members of the public who are paid to give full-time attention to duties which are incumbent on every citizen in the interest of community welfare.
> —Sir Robert Peel, Founder, London Metropolitan Police

Sir Robert made sure that his "bobbies" adhered to those principles during his tenure as London police chief. They are at the heart of what eventually came to be known as community policing in late twentieth-century America. Many American police chiefs followed that philosophy of policing in the late nineteenth and early twentieth centuries until police departments became overwhelmed by the corruption of political machine politics of many major cities. Ironically, it was a reform movement focused on the police that resulted in the unintended consequences of the police becoming alienated from the communities they were sworn to protect.

Under the principles established by Sir Robert Peel, the primary police function was crime prevention by virtue of their conspicuous presence throughout the community and their interaction with citizens. Arrest was more of a tool than a function. Urban police performed a number of social services, including setting up soup lines and referring children for needed services.

As American cities grew, so did the influence of political machines governing from smoke-filled rooms. The police became integrated with machine

41

politics and were used as instruments of control and influence. Corruption began to permeate police departments, and brutality became an enforcement tool against minorities and immigrants. Calls for reform began to grow.

The police reform movement allied itself with the progressive movement and managed to implement management practices that persisted until the late twentieth century. To be fair, there were many beneficial aspects of this strategy. The police were now to become professional crime fighters and removed from politics as civil service employees. This reduced corruption and gained favor with the public. Police abuses were reduced as evidenced by the number of Supreme Court decisions supporting police criminal investigations. The new strategy also had some severe shortcomings.

In 1910, Frederick Taylor published *The Principles of Scientific Management*. Taylor's management concepts had a major impact on management in all organizations, including the police. Science held a great mystique in the early twentieth century and thus many reformers embraced applying these principles to policing based on the term "scientific."

Taylor's management principles established clear and distinct lines between layers of management and workers. The worker's jobs were to perform certain standardized routine tasks as dictated and instructed by management. Workers were thought of as easily replaceable and dependent on management (the thinkers and planners) for instructions. Efficiency was paramount above all.

Police now became professional crime fighters focused on pursuing and capturing murderers, rapists, robbers, and other major criminals. They would no longer focus on their service and order aspect of their jobs. Professional social workers would do this.

As technology increased, police departments acquired more cars with two-way radios and took officers off the streets and into cars. The hallmark of good policing changed from a proactive model to a reactive one of responding to crimes in the shortest time possible. Efficiency in response times increased, but the police, now cruising through the community instead of being part of it, became further detached from its citizens.

As disorder increased in large American cities, the reactive policing of the past several decades began to show its vulnerabilities. More "broken windows" began to appear in American cities, and the police seemed powerless to intervene. Crime and disorder brought cries from citizens for help. Politicians responded in the only way they knew how: they enacted more laws and amended existing ones.

Academics and other experts debated about the purpose of those laws. Should we simply punish people, or should we try to get to the root causes of crime? Those root causes were identified as poverty, drug abuse, and other social ills directed at society at large. According to this notion, our society was responsible for creating the social conditions that created the problem. Growing wealth inequality was at the core of the problem. Now society was reacting to this self-made monster by punishing its victims—the offenders.

Many progressive experts argued that the growing disorder in our cities and the outcries to do something about it pitted rich against poor and white against black. But, as an example, the New York City subway customers who complained about the growing disorder in the subways were not rich. The rich have other options and don't tend to use public transportation. Working people who use public transportation complained the loudest because they wanted to commute in a clean and orderly environment.

Likewise, most people who complained about street prostitution were not prudish religious fundamentalists. They were citizens who were upset with the offensive behavior of hookers and johns committing sexual acts in parked cars, discarding condoms and needles on sidewalks, parks, and other public areas where children play.[34]

Police were the closest to the everyday problems of crime and disorder. Their instincts were not to advocate passing more sentencing laws or bother with other esoteric and philosophical concerns. Based on their everyday observations, police had always been pragmatists in their work. It was time to change their internal operating practices and procedures. Although there were dissenting voices within the ranks of the police, a few farsighted leaders decided that it was time for new strategies.

The demand for a new type of policing and a new strategy to confront crime and disorder began in many cities, but in New York, the new strategy transformed the city and gained international attention. In New York City, citizens and businesses that were fed up with crime and disorder at their doorsteps began to organize and demand action from the police and from city leaders. Private corporations and businesses began to form business improvement districts (BIDs), which invested capital in community improvement and restoration projects.

BIDs in New York worked to create crime-free public spaces based on the Broken Windows Theory. In the 1970s, Bryant Park near Times Square was taken over by the homeless, drug dealers, prostitutes, and other petty criminals. The Bryant Park Restoration Corporation (BPRC), later changed to Bryant Park Corporation (BPC), transformed the park into what today is described as an "urban jewel." The BPRC instituted a rigorous program to clean the park, remove graffiti, and repair the broken physical plant. BPRC also created a private security staff to confront unlawful behavior immediately. In addition, the Times Square Business Improvement District was instrumental in transforming Times Square into a safe and secure area for residents and tourists.

The transformation of policing in New York City took many interesting twists and turns and had a history of fits and starts in the 1980s and 1990s. One could say, however, that the transformative seed was planted by the New York Transit Authority Police Department (NYTAPD) and took root under the leadership of William Bratton, who became chief in April 1990.

In the 1980s, the subways in New York and its stations had become hovels for scores of homeless, vagrants, and petty criminals. The problem was not addressed because social scientists viewed the problem from a wrong perspective, and the police thought it was beyond their power and authority to control. The problem was viewed as part of the societal problem of homelessness, which was caused primarily by lack of affordable housing. The police viewed their mission in terms of fighting crime rather than controlling disorder.

Ridership in the New York City subways had declined sharply because riders felt intimidated and unsafe. Social service agencies and faith groups had made the situation worse with good intentions. Scores of volunteers delivered food and clothing to the homeless, who had transformed the subway system into makeshift shelters. Many of the homeless would discard their donated clothing and containers of fast food into enormous piles of foul rubbish within the stations. Others used both the cars and the stations as toilets, creating not only a nuisance but also a health hazard.

Any attempt by the police to confront disorderly behavior was immediately labeled as police harassment of the poor. This was, after all, a problem of society at large failing to provide adequate housing and care for some of its citizens. The police were frustrated at any attempt to confront the problem, but more importantly, they had bigger fish to fry as part of their job of catching criminals. Dealing with the homeless was for social workers, not cops.

In 1989, a group was commissioned by Robert Kiley, chairman of the board of the Metropolitan Transportation Authority (MTA), and David

Gunn, president of the New York City Transit Authority (NYCTA), in order to study the problem. They also named George L. Kelling as advisor to the group. Kelling, together with James Q. Wilson, had earlier introduced the Broken Windows Theory in an article in the *Atlantic Monthly* in 1982.

The group set about to study and define the problem and came up with a surprising discovery. The problem was more than just a homeless problem. As George Kelling states:

> While homelessness was a factor that aggravated the situation in the subway, few genuinely homeless individuals sought refuge there. The most significant problem was outrageous and illegal behavior by a relatively large population of subway users, some of whom appeared to be homeless but many of whom were not, a high proportion of whom were severe alcohol and drug abusers and/or seriously mentally ill, and many of whom were using the subway as a shelter.[35]

The MTA changed its rules for subway riders to prohibit specific *behaviors* rather than target an individual's *economic condition*. This was very important in overcoming legal challenges from homeless advocates that the police were targeting poor people and minorities. As an example, the previous rule against "obstructing" was changed to prohibiting "lying down." Obstructing was too broad and open to interpretation and therefore vulnerable to court action.

Other rules were adopted to prohibit applying graffiti, farebeating or tampering with fare collection boxes and turnstiles, solicitation, begging and panhandling, drinking alcoholic beverages or entering a transit facility or subway car while unable to function safely due to influence of drugs or alcohol, and several others. The legal staff from the TPD then cooperated with prosecutors' offices to develop enforcement policies.

The new rules survived legal challenges and during that period of court action were not fully implemented until William Bratton became chief of the TPD in April 1990. Bratton immediately set about transforming the TPD into a force that reflected the new and clear sense of mission, principles, and values of an agency dedicated to crime prevention through order maintenance.

The new strategy paid off almost immediately. Police discovered that many people arrested for jumping subway turnstiles were carrying weapons or narcotics or had outstanding warrants for more serious crimes.

In 1994, newly elected mayor Rudi Giuliani appointed William Bratton commissioner of the NYPD. Bratton set about transforming the NYPD with the same zeal he had shown while chief of the TPD. His Broken Windows Theory of order maintenance guided his policies. The new mission for the police was to prevent crimes through problem solving. They were to be considered part of the communities they served and collaborated with citizens, businesses, and other justice components and other city agencies.

As in the subway system, the focus was on addressing "quality of life" offenses that devastate communities and create the conditions for crime to flourish. He began with a new notion of community policing. In the 1980s and early 1990s, the term "community policing" was not fully or universally defined. Those departments that practiced community policing did so by designating a particular unit or group of officers as "community police" (a practice that remains to this day in some departments). Their work was generally couched in terms of "soft on crime" strategies that emphasized social work and maintaining friendly relations with the community. The rest of the department practiced "real" police work. This distinction persists in many police departments to this day.

Bratton infused the entire NYPD with a new and clear sense of mission that focused on tending to small problems (crimes that had previously been considered petty or merely a nuisance) before they became big problems. His notion of community policing could best be described as problem-oriented policing (POP) because of its emphasis on problem solving.

Bratton reorganized the NYPD's organizational structure to empower precinct commanders as well as individual patrol officers to make decisions. He held meetings with precinct commanders twice weekly to report on progress and to assess future trends and develop strategies. He later used a computer-driven process that came to be called COMPSTAT (computer statistics or comparative statistics) to determine trends in crimes and arrests in various parts of the city. COMPSTAT gave the department an indication of the types and number of crimes occurring in different neighborhoods. This aided in developing tactics and strategies to confront and solve those problems.

The new strategies of both the NYPD and TPD began paying off. As with the experience in the subway system, the NYPD discovered that people arrested for such minor crimes as urinating in public or vandalism were often carrying illegal weapons, narcotics, or had outstanding warrants for more serious crimes. There were other unexpected consequences.

In 1996, John Royster was arrested for brutal attacks on four women over a period of several days. The crime might not have been solved but for the fact that fingerprints recovered at one of the crime scenes matched those taken from Royster when he was arrested three months earlier for a low-level offense of jumping a subway turnstile.[36]

This method of proactive policing has since spread to virtually every major metropolitan police department in the country. The beneficial results have exceeded the expectations of many professionals. The anti-incarceration lobby, however, struggles to make sense of dropping crime rates and turn it to their advantage.

The NYPD's tactics and strategies have drawn a chorus of caustic criticism from critics who advocate more reactive measures like shorter and less severe sentencing. The great irony is that proactive policing has reduced crime and thus reduced incarceration.

In a *New York Post* article, Heather MacDonald from the Manhattan Institute writes:

> Foes of New York City's proactive style of policing struggle mightily to downplay its most obvious benefit: the largest crime drop on record, concentrated overwhelmingly in minority neighborhoods. Now they have a new challenge: ignoring the fact that assertive NYPD policing also lowers the prison population.
>
> A new study from two top liberal criminologists, Michael Jacobson and James Austin, suggests that the way to decrease incarceration without increasing crime is through more law enforcement, not less.[37]

Critics like to play the race card when criticizing proactive police tactics, claiming that such practices unfairly target minorities. The problem is they focus on the wrong victims—the offenders—while ignoring that the real victims—law-abiding minority residents in low-income neighborhoods—are safer now than twenty years ago.

The increased patrols and arrests by the NYPD in public housing for trespassers benefits the law-abiding residents by preventing crimes most often committed by trespassers. The trespasser at most will be sent to Rikers Island jail for trespassing rather than to a state prison for a more serious crime.

The state of Texas is a model that the anti-incarceration lobby holds up to illustrate that when a state reduces incarceration, it can do so while reducing crime. The only problem is that they've put the cart before the horse. Because of proactive, problem-oriented policing in its major cities and a more proactive justice system, the Texas crime rate has plunged, thereby eliminating the need for more incarceration.

Many Texas jurisdictions such as Dallas and Austin practice community prosecution. The corrections department in Texas also has a public safety focus and the probation department (community supervision) is very proactive in working with the community and addressing problems. This is because of forward thinking leaders, such as Dan Beto, the retired Founding Director of the Correctional Management Institute of Texas (CMIT) at Sam Houston State University. I'll describe community prosecution as well the new probation in later chapters.

Anti-incarceration advocates nonetheless persist on publishing studies and articles inferring that fewer prisoners equal less crime. This secondary strategy is equally disingenuous. I think the absurdity of asking why prisons are full *despite* a drop in crime has finally dawned on them.

I'm afraid however that this is wishful thinking.

The most important thing to note is that the anti-incarceration lobby is exactly that—a lobby. It exists to influence politicians to pass more "progressive" sentencing laws that will (in their view) reduce incarceration. Employing experts to conduct studies and write papers and articles about the harmful effects of mass incarceration is one of their most valuable tools.

The proactive strategy of community policing had an influence on all other justice components in the 1990s. The courts, probation, prosecution, and institution corrections began to be more community oriented. It's hard to say whether the other components began to change their strategies *because* of community policing, but the criminal justice revolution began with the police. One thing that *can* be said is that, like the NYPD, the changes occurred because of the department changing is own internal policies, not because of new laws that were passed by the legislature.

This new way of doing justice may threaten to render the anti-incarceration lobby irrelevant. Maybe this is what frightens them.

CHAPTER 5

Holding Court in and with the Community

In his book, *Guilty: The Collapse of Criminal Justice*, Judge Harold J. Rothwax, New York State Supreme Court justice, states:

> If you were to visit my courtroom on any given Wednesday, you would see the passing parade of our justice system as you have never seen it on television and the movies. Wednesday is calendar day. That means there is no regular trial in session ... we try to dispose of cases, ready them for hearings and trials, and impose sentences on those cases where the defendant has been found guilty or has pleaded guilty. Today, there are ninety-four cases on the docket. I have the details of each one handwritten on an index card, and I begin arranging the cards across the desk according to their status. It's an old-fashioned system, but it has always served me well.[38]

If the main function of the traditional justice system is to process cases, the best look at this sausage factory at work is through the lens of our courts. An endless parade of defendants from drunk drivers to mass murderers begins the process at arraignment through conviction and sentencing.

Along the factory's conveyer belt, pretrial officers, public defenders, and prosecutors examine defendants and their cases. Step into the offices of any one of these professionals and you're apt to find the occupants hidden behind stacks of cases.

The bad news for the public, but specifically for victims, is that the system is not about protecting their interests. It's about seeing that the state gets compensated for any wrongdoing and the defendant's (offender) rights are not violated. Convicted offenders are held accountable, but the state, or "the people," is viewed as the victim. It's an adversarial system in which the defense and prosecution battle each other not so much for the truth, but to win.

Processing cases as expediently as possible makes plea-bargaining an essential tool. This means that offenders often end up serving time for offenses less serious than those they actually committed. The courts, as well as the police, are ruled by criminal procedure law, which is designed to protect the rights of the accused. Defense attorney's often misuse and manipulate these essential rules. The result is that the guilty can be let off on a technicality.

An attorney would say that when it comes to the constitution, there's no such thing as a technicality. I would only cite the following example from New York:

> [Philip] Conner was arrested and charged with assault in the second degree and thereafter released on bail. The district attorney subsequently informed Conner's attorney that he had been indicted, and the defense attorney selected the date when he and Conner would appear for arraignment. They arrived that morning and were told that the case would not be called until later that afternoon. Since Conner's attorney had other cases to attend to, they left the courtroom. It is quite common for defense attorneys to have numerous cases calendared different court parts on the same day.
>
> Conner's case was again adjourned to a mutually agreeable date. On that date, Conner's attorney was on trial in another matter and he sent his law partner in his stead. Conner and his attorney slid into the back row of the courtroom and sat there without informing anyone of their presence. Strictly speaking, this is legal; ethically it's questionable. At the very least, it's a form of game playing that many defense attorneys engage in. It worked for Conner. Inadvertently, Conner's case was not called.

The two delays in Conner's case were charged to the state, and because they exceeded by three days the six-month speedy trial provision, the indictment was dismissed. Conner walked.[39]

This is only one of countless instances that take place everyday in our nation's court system. There's little regard for the actual victim of the crime because the crime, in theory, was committed against the state. Ultimately, the state's interest is what drives the process.

The development of this system has been a long and slow process dating back to Anglo-Saxon England. In order to better understand it, we have to examine its roots. Under Anglo-Saxon law, an offense was considered to be committed against an individual victim rather than our present system where an offense is against the state or "the people." The important consequence of this distinction was that offenders were forced to compensate their victims. Anglo-Saxon society was comprised of small tribal groups. Elders and chieftains enforced order and compliance to the rules within the tribe.

If a powerful offender resisted tribal justice, the victim could call upon an earl or king for enforcement. When this happened, and if found guilty, the offender could be forced to pay not only the victim but also the earl or king who enforced the settlement. Eventually, kings began to see a cash cow in the justice process. More and more offenses became declared as not against an individual victim but against "the king's peace." The evolution of law moved from one of torts (causing harm to an individual that required compensation) to one of crimes harming the state or king. Whereas the spoils of tort law were awarded to the individual victim, the spoils of criminal law went to the king.

After the Norman conquest of England in 1066, the list of offenses against the king's peace grew larger. The important thing is that the basis of our justice system maintains the notion that crimes are committed against the state rather than individual victims. This explains the traditional lack of concern of the system for victims' needs. As I've stated, victims are only useful to the state in helping convict the offender in the name of the state or "the people."[40]

This design flaw, if you will, in the system is what gave birth to and drives the current victims' rights movement. It also spawned the restorative justice movement. Restorative justice is a method of responding to crime by first acknowledging that crimes are committed against individual victims and that the aim of justice should be to restore the victim to the highest degree possible. Victims take an active role in the process, while offenders are encouraged to take responsibility for their actions by repairing the harm they've done through apologizing, returning stolen money, or community service.

Restorative justice brings an old concept—victim restoration—and makes it new and relevant to modern times. Many of its values and principles were incorporated into what have come to be known as community courts.

The old English proverb that says, "Necessity is the mother of invention," can be applied to the birth of community courts. The first community court was established in New York City. The Manhattan Midtown Community Court was established in 1993 at the height of New York City's crime and disorder epidemic.

The "broken windows" effect had infested the city's neighborhoods but, most importantly, two of the city's primary tourist attractions—Times Square and the theater district. It was impossible for people to walk the primary thoroughfares, Forty-Second Street and Broadway, without being accosted by aggressive panhandlers, drunks, and various con artists or dope dealers. Among the garbage on the streets, one might pass by homeless and other vagrants urinating in the streets or alleys.

New York was considered a city in crisis, and many thought it was ungovernable. The early 1990s was the height of the crack cocaine epidemic in America's cities. Many of the residential stoops in the midtown Manhattan area had become crack emporiums where people sat and sold crack.

The street people, petty criminals, and other undesirables had taken control of the streets from the citizens that lived and worked in the neighborhood. Tourists began to shy away from Broadway shows. Residents and local business owners expressed a fear that things were out of control. One of their primary questions was "Where were the police?"

Judith S. Kay, chief judge of the State of New York, expressed the shared frustration. "It troubles me as a judge. It troubles me as a lawyer. It troubles me as a wife and mother and grandmother, that the justice system has suffered such an enormous erosion of public trust and confidence."[41]

The police, meanwhile, were doing what they perceived to be their jobs—catching bad guys. By "bad guys," they meant violent criminals like murderers, rapists, and armed robbers. If a cop saw someone urinating on the sidewalk or passed out at the entrance to a business or residence, he would choose not to bother because his job was to catch "real criminals." Besides, if he *did* make an arrest, the courts were so overwhelmed with cases that it would be dismissed. So why even bother?

The courts, as well as our entire criminal justice system, were designed with different perceptions and types of thinking about justice that ignored the current realities of crime and disorder in our communities. With the increasing deterioration of order and desperate cries for help from embattled citizens, it was time to reinvent the system.

The important question that first needed to be asked was "Who was the victim?" Many of the petty crimes, such as street prostitution, were considered "victimless." It was nonetheless becoming clear that the victim was the community—the residents, the businesses, and the entire neighborhood. Crime and disorder had become a matter of survival for the business community as well as the community as a whole.

In 1993, a combination of business owners, residents, and forward-thinking criminal justice officials began to rethink the purpose of the system—more specifically, the value of the system to it's "customers," the community. The Times Square Business Improvement District (BID), a private group of property owners and commercial tenants, joined the court system and other criminal justice agencies to establish the Midtown Manhattan Community Court, or simply the Midtown Community Court.

The Midtown Community Court is based on a radical notion of justice that specifically focuses on quality-of-life crimes. These are the types of crimes that chip away at a community's soul and begin the decay from within by producing more serious crime. The court is based on an old idea that crime should have consequences and the victim (the community) must be paid back.

Robert G.M. Keating, administrative judge, states:

> One of the major drives behind the Midtown Community Court was a sense on the part of Court Administrators like myself and others that in essence our criminal court was becoming irrelevant in helping communities solve their quality of life offenses. The idea that we have is one of restorative justice; one in which defendants pay back the community by very visible work from a defendant who basically has no money and has nothing other than personal service to pay with.[42]

Defendants are tried and sentenced on the same day of arrest. Their sentence consists of community service, where they clean up graffiti, pick up trash off the streets, plant trees, and other neighborhood improvement. The court also provides other services on site, such as drug treatment, education, and health services. The philosophy is that swift reaction offers more effective treatment.

The court has helped addicts get clean and has helped prostitutes get off the streets and away from their abusive pimps. It helps ex-cons with job skills, including preparing for job interviews. This is the result of combining immediate punishment and treatment.

The establishment of the Midtown Court also offered the police an incentive to arrest low-level, quality-of-life offenders. The results were immediate, as with community policing in general. Low-level offenders often commit more serious crimes, and their arrest on a low-level offense often yields bigger rewards. Many of these offenders have outstanding warrants for other offenses or are found in possession of weapons or narcotics.

Once a month, law enforcement, prosecutors, defense attorneys, business owners, and residents meet to discuss policy and advise the court on progress. This advisory board of citizens and justice officials makes this system of "community" justice radically different from the traditional criminal justice system.

The result has been a transformation of the Times Square area. If you take a walk down Broadway after dark, you're apt to find people with children strolling down the street and walking into family friendly shops and restaurants. This is a big change from the peep shows, pimps, prostitutes, dope dealers, and other street people of the past.

The idea of a community court hasn't been lost on other parts of the city or of the country. The Red Hook section of Brooklyn suffered the devastating effects of the crack cocaine and heroine epidemic of the 1970s and 1980s. This neighborhood was plagued by unemployment, poverty, and crime. In 1992, a turning point was the tragic murder of a school principal who was looking for a truant student. The community decided that enough was enough.

Chief Judge Judith S. Kaye, who was instrumental in establishing the Midtown Community Court, developed the concept for a community court in Red Hook. In the spring of 2000, the Red Hook Community Justice Center opened in a renovated Catholic school. It focuses on the same community quality of issues as the Midtown Community Court, but one thing that stands out (although not unique to this court) is the fact that the prosecution and defense are part of the same team in terms of wanting the same outcome. Brett Taylor, defense attorney with the Legal Aid Society says:

> If you don't have a system like this that is trying to offer the help, trying to give the help; a lot of time these people they're going to be in jail for thirty days and then they'll go right back into the environment that put them there in the first place.[43]

That sentiment is echoed by Prosecutor Gerianne Abriano:

> A lot of what we do here is essentially trying to help the defendants overcome their drug dependency or some other problems that they may have with the goal of getting them to lead crime free lives.[44]

These truly radical statements by two different people, who in our traditional criminal justice system are in adversarial positions, turn our entire notion of justice on its head.

Judge Alex Calabrese of the Community Justice Center makes an interesting observation:

> Sometimes a court has to use jail as a tool just like the treatment is used as a tool ... and it's sometimes that short jail period that really gets the person to understand that if he or she continues down that road this is exactly where it's going to get you.[45]

The idea behind these statements is truly revolutionary. They're at the heart of the "quiet revolution" occurring in criminal justice.

The Midtown Community Court gave rise to the Center for Court Innovation. This is a public/private partnership between the New York State Unified Court System and the Fund for the City of New York. Its mission is to help the justice system aid victims, reduce crime, strengthen neighborhoods, and improve public trust in justice. Through its work, the center has spread the concept of community courts throughout the country and the world.

Community courts have given rise to other problem-solving courts that specialize in specific offenses, such as domestic violence and drug abuse. Critics maintain that too much specialization can hinder justice efforts by creating a new and more complicated maze for just about every single offense rather than the one-stop shop of community courts. At this time, this remains to be seen.

The important lesson is the realization that jail and treatment (punishment and rehabilitation) are tools that are a means to an end. This is what escapes the awareness of so many experts. For too long, the discussion about criminal justice policy has been a continuous debate between punishment and rehabilitation, with each side trying to change the debate to their own advantage. The new criminal justice embodied in community policing, community courts, and the other justice components don't try to change the debate. They end it.

CHAPTER 6

Prosecuting the Victimizers, Helping the Victims

Portland, Oregon, in the 1980s was, like every major city in the country, a place where quality-of-life crimes received little or no priority or resources. Many of the most crime-prone neighborhoods had large numbers of drug houses where dealers and manufacturers of illegal substances operated with little or no fear of arrest and prosecution. Public trust and confidence in the justice system by residents and business owners in these neighborhoods was at an all-time low.

In 1990, following the success of community policing in Portland, Multnomah County District Attorney Michael Schrunk began to explore ways in which the office of the district attorney might shift its services based on the success of the community-policing model. A task force was formed within a Portland business and residential district, concerned about public safety and "livability" issues. Its purpose was to study ways in which the district might better address those issues.

The task force provided a structure for the district attorney's office to use a combination of public and private resources to fund a pilot community-prosecution project. The project would eventually be called the Neighborhood DA Program and was expanded in 1992 to other neighborhoods in Portland.

The DA's office partnered with the police, citizens, and social service agencies and formed a public safety committee in order to develop problem-solving strategies. Of particular concern to the neighborhood police and residents was the revolving-door nature of the criminal justice system that allowed drug dealers to return, within hours of their arrests, to the neighborhoods where they had committed the crimes.

A plan to create drug-free zones was developed by working with the city government. The Public Safety Committee met to ensure that they agreed on the concept of drug-free zones before they approached the city council with the policy proposal. Once this agreement was obtained, the district attorney's office organized drug-free zones under a city ordinance prohibiting trespassing. If a person was arrested on a drug-related charge within the drug-free zone, they could not return to the streets or sidewalks within that zone without violating the ordinance. If they did, they'd be subject to arrest for trespass. Zone violators' pictures were attached to zone violation cards, which included the time period that offenders were banned from the particular zone. Copies of these cards were distributed to residents, beat cops, and social service providers within drug-free zones, as well as surrounding areas, to combat repeat offenders.

According to the district attorney's office, the implementation of the drug-free zone ordinance has been an effective tool in deterring drug trafficking because district police officers can arrest zone violators simply for trespassing. Dealers fear the strategy because they run the risk of forfeiting any drugs in their possessions at the time of arrest.[46]

The district attorney's office also implemented creative ways of closing down neighborhood drug houses. The most effective way to determine if a building or residence is being used for drug trafficking is by executing a search warrant. The police can gather evidence of criminal activity that can be used by a landlord to evict a problem tenant or by the city to close the house. However, drug houses don't sell the large amounts of drugs that justify intense, time-consuming felony investigations. It's also a fact that many drug house operators don't sell drugs to police informants. This makes obtaining traditional search warrants difficult and sometimes impossible.

This led the office to involve the community in resolving its own problems. They used citizen's observations to establish probable cause for search warrant affidavits. These "community warrants" are now used by police to close down neighborhood drug houses. Neighbors can also anonymously report how many people come and go and how often, plus many other indicators of a drug house.

An important factor is that police corroborate what neighbors say. If the suspected illegal activity can't be corroborated, a warrant is not requested.

This illustrates the power of collaboration between the justice components and the communities they serve. The Neighborhood Deputy District Attorneys (NDDA) are assigned to work directly in the Multnomah County neighborhoods that they serve. The NDDA has offices at local police agency precincts. This is what a system that's not only in the community but is also a part of the community looks like.

Manhattan Community Prosecution

In his 1985 reelection campaign, District Attorney Robert Morgenthau promised to introduce a long-term, community-based strategy for crime prevention and prosecution. The Manhattan district attorney's office has a long history of encouraging partnerships between the police and community members in order to prevent and confront crime. Community policing was an emerging concept that was starting to take root in many cities in the country. Strong bonds of collaboration were forming between the police and the community, but prosecutors played no role in these partnerships.

The district attorney's office decided to fill this void by creating a strategy combining the efforts of prosecutors, police, and communities "to identify crime patterns proactively, develop solutions which prevent crime and ensure swift and certain judgment, implement these solutions, and measure the resulting impact on the community."[47] This strategy, emphasizing cooperation between prosecutors, police, and community members, became the New York County District Attorney's Office Community Prosecution Program.

The Community Affairs Unit (CAU) is one of eight components in the program that contributes to the overall mission of crime prevention through community partnerships. It works with police precincts, block associations, tenants groups, landlords, schools, business improvement districts, and religious institutions in teaching citizens how to assist the criminal justice system in preventing crime.

A director, deputy director, six community associates, and two staff assistants staff the CAU. It is divided into two teams, representing northern and southern Manhattan. Each CAU staff member is assigned to a particular geographic area, consisting of one or more police precincts, and is responsible for maintaining community relationships within their area. CAU staff members meet regularly with community members in neighborhoods, schools, churches, or at local police precincts.

They work with several law enforcement agencies, including local NYPD police precincts, the New York City Narcotics Division, the transit authority police, and the housing authority police, along with state and federal agencies. They also work with other city agencies, such as the Department of Probation, the Department of Sanitation, or the community board, to target drug crime in a specific area.

The other seven components within the program also work with citizens and police to develop creative strategies to confront crime at the neighborhood level. One of these components is the Narcotics Eviction Program, which has worked to close down drug houses by helping owners evict drug-dealing tenants by using civil laws that had seldom been used before.

In 2014, after murder reached a low point in Manhattan, the district attorney's office and the NYPD began to collaborate to attack other crimes, such as grand larceny, domestic violence, and cybercrime.

In 2014, District Attorney Cyrus Vance and Police Commissioner William Bratton teamed up senior prosecutors and police commanders to devise strategies for targeting the main perpetrators of these particular crimes. They used the same intelligence-gathering techniques that were used by the DA's office to dismantle street gangs.

A creative funding source for the project was more than twenty million dollars from drug forfeiture cases to pay for new technology. The money was invested in fiber-optic information systems and handheld tablets that provide information to police officers about suspects.

The partnership allows police to focus on more specific types of offenses because of a major decline in major violent crimes in the city.

The number of murders in Manhattan fell to thirty-nine in 2013, down from seventy in 2010, when District Attorney Vance took office, and the lowest since reliable record-keeping began in 1962, according to the state division of criminal justice services reports. Shooting episodes declined over the same period to 115 from 146. Police statistics show rapes and robberies also fell significantly in Manhattan since 2010, while assaults and larcenies ticked upward.[48]

Denver's Community Justice Councils

Since launching its community prosecution program in 1996, the Denver District Attorney's Office has come up with creative ways of doing more on a limited budget. They've done this primarily by encouraging the community to play an active leadership role. One of the Denver DA's first initiatives was to establish community justice councils. The councils bring citizens together to set priorities and develop new problem-solving strategies. They work through community accountability boards, which use community volunteers to determine responses to youth crime and through a community court.

Each council has twenty to thirty-five members that are chosen by community prosecutors through in-depth interviews, and each council is formed within different neighborhoods. Council members consist of residents, business leaders, community center directors, faith leaders, school-teachers, community police officers, prosecutors, and elected city and state representatives. One of the benefits is that some quality-of-life issues are resolved without formal action by the state or city prosecutor.

One important aspect is that not all neighborhoods need community justice councils. In neighborhoods with low crime and greater community social structures, it makes more sense to offer support and assistance rather than having the district attorney's office create a new structure and giving the impression that government knows best by replacing the supports already in place.[49]

I've described only a few projects, but community prosecution has spread throughout the country. Each program is unique to the districts they serve, but they all share common principles. They each demonstrate that justice components working in concert with one another and with the community for a common purpose creates a vital energy that can confront and subdue crime.

CHAPTER 7

Reinventing Probation

In 1841, John Augustus, a prosperous Boston shoemaker, was in court when an officer brought in a prisoner. The prisoner was charged being a common drunkard, and Augustus, who was a member of the temperance movement, was there to bail him out.

Augustus was determined to help the prisoner and save him from the house of correction. He convinced the judge to release him to his care for a probationary period of time. When the prisoner returned to court three weeks later for sentencing, accompanied by Augustus, the judge was astonished by the prisoner's transformation in appearance and demeanor.

Thus began the work of "the father of probation." For the remainder of his life, Augustus convinced the courts to release hundreds of individuals to his care.

For the next 150 years, the framework established by John Augustus dominated the practice of probation. The purpose of probation was to help people avoid prison by helping them overcome their problems. A system that was designed to help alcoholics and other afflicted individuals began to develop a split personality as more and more probationers were charged with serious crimes, including homicide and rape. Were probation officers supposed to be social workers or cops or both? In 2012, according to the Bureau of Justice Statistics, 53 percent of probationers were on probation for felonies and 19 percent for violent offenses.

Regardless of this, the operating principles of probation remained focused on the offender (often referred to as "the client"). Some of these attitudes remain to this day but are rapidly changing. Experts have been telling probation officers that their (sole) mission is to provide more effective treatment and supervision of the offender. Effective supervision is based on the latest trends regarding electronic monitoring or better assessment of risks posed to the public based on scientific measurements and tools. The ultimate goal is to reduce recidivism, meaning, helping the offender avoid incarceration.

In the early 1990s, some forward-thinking probation officials began to examine what the purpose of probation should be. One function of probation was (and is) an inducement for plea-bargaining, but it failed to address the public's rage and frustration over its mounting fear of crime. Probation's steadfast focus on the offender as the sole client, whether for rehabilitation or supervision, had created a crisis of confidence in its ability to perform its mission. But what exactly was or should be the mission of probation?

Some chief probation officers began to embrace the concept of restorative justice because of its emphasis on victim restitution. Restitution to victims had become a bad joke. For more than two decades, judges had ordered more restitution payments because of political pressure from victims' rights advocates, but collecting it was a different matter.

After offenders paid their fines, probation officers often asked the court to withdraw restitution for their clients. After all, offenders were seen as destitute victims of drug abuse and other problems who couldn't be expected to pay restitution.

In the early 1990s, the nation was becoming more aware of the insidious problem of domestic violence. More abusers were being placed on probation for injuring and terrorizing the victims they didn't kill. Most were sentenced for simple misdemeanor assaults or violations of restraining orders. Probation officers did what they were supposed to do—order the abuser into treatment. Their main interest was on the rehabilitation of the offender rather than on protecting the victim. This created the potential for a homicide.

George Lardner Jr. wrote about the murder of his daughter by a Massachusetts probationer in 1992. His story is an indictment of probation and the criminal justice system in general. The mission of probation was to make the offender go to treatment, not to protect Lardner's daughter or anyone else from the probationer. When informed that the probationer was abusing a new victim, the probation department's response was to intensify its pressure to get him into treatment.[50]

Restorative justice shifted the focus toward restoring the victim for the harm caused by the perpetrator, but it was missing some vital elements. For one thing, restorative justice was seen as a reactive response to crime—a very innovative response, but a response nonetheless. A crime had to be committed and produce a victim before any restorative practices could be applied.

Restorative justice also adhered to much of the narrative of traditional criminal justice reform. The present system was considered retributive, meaning that punishment was the sole or primary response based on the high number of incarcerated individuals.

With the growing awareness of domestic violence, a big flaw in restorative justice was its emphasis on victim-offender reconciliation or mediation. In many cases, this is a worthy goal, but in domestic violence, the ultimate goal is to protect the victim rather than to reconcile both parties or mediate their disputes. Something closer related to the principles of community policing and community courts was needed. In essence, it was time for a new paradigm of justice and probation.

In 2000, the American Probation and Parole Association put forth a position statement on "community justice." The position statement is perhaps the most comprehensive interpretation of the new justice paradigm. It defines community justice as "a strategic method of crime reduction and prevention, which builds or enhances partnerships within communities." And its mission is to "confront crime and delinquency through proactive, problem-solving practices aimed at prevention, control, reduction and reparation of the harm crime has caused."

It also proclaimed that the community was the primary "customer" of the system. Community members pay for the system through their taxes and are thus entitled to a system that serves their interests first and foremost.[51]

Contemporary probation just wasn't up to the task of meeting the demands by the public for safer and more secure communities. This realization led to innovated thinking on the part of probation executives.

In March 1997, a meeting was held at the Manhattan Institute in New York to assess the state of probation and to discuss ideas for its reinvention. Academicians and probation executives from around the country attended the meeting. A reinventing probation council was subsequently formed, headed by Ronald P. Corbett, Jr., second deputy commissioner from Massachusetts probation.

The council also included Rick Faulkner, a colleague from NIC. Rick, a former federal probation officer, and I shared the same views about the problems with our criminal justice system. We were a distinct minority.

One revolutionary conclusion from the council was that probation needed to look in the mirror to assign blame for its problems. Probation and corrections in general tend to blame outside forces for its problems. There are never enough resources provided by politicians and never enough support from the public. If probation is to avoid irrelevance, it should transform itself from within instead of remaining a perpetual victim of outside powers beyond its control.

The Broken Windows Theory served as the blueprint for reinventing probation. Probation should adopt the problem-solving strategies of community policing and form partnerships with police, community members, and organizations, as well as other justice components.

The idea of probation and police partnerships was especially revolutionary. Historically, probation and police have worked at cross-purposes. Probation officers view their mission as keeping their clients out of prison, while police are viewed as trying to arrest their clients and send them to prison. "Broken windows probation" provided a common mission for probation, police, and the entire justice system based on the principles of community justice.

Massachusetts had been a pioneer of problem-solving probation since the early 1990s. During this time, the probation department in Quincy, Massachusetts, began to regard domestic violence victims as important clients. Domestic violence was considered not only a crime against a specific victim but also a crime against the community.

They developed a domestic-violence program dedicated to breaking the cycle of violence and protecting the victim. It became a model for domestic-violence programs nationally and internationally. Batterers may be sentenced to community work service and to batterer-specific treatment.

Probation works collaboratively with the police and other agencies to identify and respond to instances of domestic violence. The most effective part of the program's principles is the understanding that batterers are very skilled at manipulating or intimidating their way back into the home of the victim after being issued a restraining order. Once a batterer reunites with the victim, the victim's chances of being killed increase exponentially.

"No contact with the victim" on restraining orders should mean exactly that—no phone calls, no birthday cards, no "accidental" meetings in public places, or any other type of contact. Probation officers therefore do not hesitate to revoke batterers who violate restraining orders, even for the slightest infraction. The ultimate goal is to protect the victim, not to keep the offender out of jail.

Drunk driving was becoming a big problem in Quincy in the early 1990s. The probation department studied the problem of how drunk drivers became drunk prior to killing someone on the highway. They found that they tended to drink at certain bars that illegally over-served alcohol to their customers. They worked with the state alcohol control agency to close down these bars. This had a positive impact on drunk-driving rates.

Other probation departments in Massachusetts have been as creative and innovative. In the early 1990s, Boston was experiencing a rash of gang violence, a rise in homicide victims under the age of seventeen, and public alarm at the increasing crime and disorder in the streets. Boston experienced seventy-five homicides and 5,920 aggravated assaults in 1987. In 1988, it rose to ninety-five homicides and 6,291 aggravated assaults. By 1990, homicides reached a high of 152 and 6,960 aggravated assaults were reported to police.[52] People on probation committed a high percentage of the violence.

There was mounting criticism of the police from the minority community. Probation officers worked independently of police, and curfews were not commonly imposed by the court and were difficult to enforce primarily because probation officers worked behind a desk in their offices from nine to five, Monday through Friday. Offenders on probation were well aware of the limited supervision capabilities of the probation department and thus took full advantage of the situation.

In response to those problems, a few probation officers met informally with a few police officers to discuss ways of addressing the gang-related problems in the city. In 1992, police received a call of a shooting in the Dorchester area of Boston. Two probation officers were on a ride-along with the police, and they arrived at the scene where a large crowd of young people was standing around the wounded body of a fifteen-year-old victim. The police stepped out of the car, and no one left the scene because there was no crime in standing around a crime scene. However, when the two probation officers stepped out of the backseat of the car, the crowd immediately began to disperse.

The victim and several of the onlookers were or had been on probation and supervised by one of the officers. They knew that being at the scene likely violated their probation. The crowd dispersal indicated that probation could exert greater control on probationers if they knew they were being watched. It also allowed many onlookers to avoid peer pressure to stay at the scene by providing them an excuse that probation officers were checking for curfew violations or area restrictions.

Out of this ride-along Operation Night Light was born. In 1993, the Boston police established a special unit to address gang violence. The unit works with the probation department, and four nights a week, teams of police and probation officers visit the homes of high-risk probationers. Churches, schools, and other community groups are part of the partnership. One positive result is that Night Light helps parents establish parental control.

If the school reports that a certain offender is falling behind in classes and isn't doing assigned homework, the parent usually says it's because the kid is out at all hours of the night. Because of strict curfew checks, the offender is not only more likely to remain at home, but it also provides him an excuse to his friends to avoid peer pressure to engage in criminal activities.

The positive impact of Operation Night Light was and continues to be remarkable. Between 1996 and 1998, the city experienced a 70 percent decrease in the number of people age twenty-four and under killed by guns. Between July 1995 and December 1997, no juvenile in Boston was killed with a firearm.[53]

Another problem with traditional probation is the issue of warrants for violations. Police have always been swamped with arrest warrants of all kinds. Probation always dumped these warrants into the pool, correctly thinking it was all that was required of them. By the time the police got around to serving the warrant, the offender may have victimized several people.

Many probation departments now allow the chief probation officer to issue temporary warrants for probation violators when going through a judge would be inconvenient, such as after hours. The court will eventually certify the warrant during regular business hours.

Some probation departments in several states have special armed units that serve warrants on certain high-risk offenders and put them in custody. This frees the police to pursue their duties and reduces the risk of victimization on the part of the offender. Many probation departments also post pictures of the "most wanted" probation violators and absconders. This allows the community to aid in their apprehension.

Probation now supervises offenders within a new framework—one in which the community and victims are clients, not just the offender. The desired outcomes are safer communities and a reduction in victimization. Probation is now at the forefront of the criminal justice revolution and no longer the "invisible giant" of corrections. Reformers have been calling for alternatives to incarceration as if probation didn't exist or was invisible. With its new role as a valued partner with the community in confronting crime, there's no turning back.

CHAPTER 8

Prisons: A New Mission That's Working

Early American colonists practiced punitive methods on offenders that were universally common at the time. Widespread practices included such things as branding and confining people in stocks on public display. These harsh methods came into conflict with the democratic ideals established by the American Revolution. Many perceived (as many perceive today) a dilemma of imprisoning individuals in a free society.

The attempt to reconcile that dilemma began with the American Quakers establishing a new type of prison in 1790—the Philadelphia Walnut Street Jail. The jail was based on a lofty goal of reforming convicts through solitary confinement and total abstinence from alcohol. The only reading material allowed was a Bible. Because the inmates performed penance through their solitude and isolation, the Walnut Street Jail was called a "Penitentiary House." Needless to say, the idea of forcing people to reform through solitary confinement failed. Many inmates reportedly went mad.[54]

The penitentiary was the outcome of a reform movement with a misplaced sense of priorities. Even though the idea was a flop, the mission for prisons was forever engraved within the lexicon of corrections. The primary mission of prisons was to "correct," reform, or rehabilitate inmates.

American prisons have been held to that measure ever since. Any attempt by politicians or administrators to establish policies that appear more punitive or controlling is immediately attacked by reformers as tampering with or abandoning the "true" mission. Prisons are held accountable if inmates are released and commit more crimes. They're called human warehouses regardless of the educational and vocational learning they provide.

Because many consider prisons incompatible with a free society (except for the most violent), it seems that nothing they do can fully redeem their usefulness. They're called "violent schools of crime," but when they clamp down on violence, they become more oppressive in the eyes of critics.

On October 22, 1983, inmate Thomas Silverstein, a member of the Aryan Brotherhood prison gang, was released from his cell in the control unit of the US penitentiary Marion to take a shower. He was shackled, but as he passed in front of another cell, an inmate slipped him a shank and an improvised handcuff key. After freeing his hands, Silverstein attacked Officer Merle Clutts and killed him by stabbing him forty times.

Later that same day, another Aryan Brotherhood member, Clayton Fountain, used the same method to kill another Marion correctional officer, Robert Hoffman. The back-to-back murders sent shock waves throughout the Bureau of Prisons. I was working at the Lewisburg Federal Penitentiary at the time, and the news cast a pall of gloom that lasted several days.

The Marion Federal Penitentiary was the most secure prison in the country and had replaced Alcatraz after it had closed in 1963. The Marion control unit was like a maximum-security unit within a maximum-security prison. It housed the most violent offenders in the system—the worst of the worse.

Thomas Silverstein and Clayton Fountain were exactly the types of inmates the unit was designed for. In 1981, they were charged with killing a black inmate at Marion by strangling him to death. Silverstein and Fountain then killed a friend of the murdered inmate who had sought to avenge his death. They reportedly stabbed the inmate sixty-seven times and then dragged his bloody corpse up and down the prison tier so other prisoners could see their handiwork.

Through these murders, Silverstein and Fountain were sending a message on behalf of the Aryan Brotherhood that no matter where you locked them up, they'd get to you. It should be noted that there was no federal death penalty at the time of these murders, and Silverstein and Fountain were already serving life sentences for murder. The Bureau of Prisons clearly got the message.

The bureau consequently locked down Marion, meaning that all inmates would be locked in their cells twenty-three hours a day. Marion thus essentially became the nation's first super-max prison. The response from angry inmate advocates was swift and expected. The Bureau of Prisons (BOP) was hit by a wave of lawsuits claiming cruel and unusual punishment.

The BOP eventually prevailed in court and set out to build a new institution specifically designed as a super-max facility. The states, meanwhile, were watching and waiting to see what would happen once the dust settled.

In 1994, the BOP announced the opening of its new administrative maximum (ADMAX) facility in Florence, Colorado. Silverstein and Fountain, meanwhile, were transferred to other federal prisons. Fountain died of a heart attack in 2004, and Silverstein is now housed at the ADMAX. Critics have been decrying the use of solitary confinement since super-max prisons began proliferating after the BOP successfully fended off all initial lawsuits.

Silverstein's account of his plight in isolation at the Atlanta penitentiary is documented in a sympathetic publication:

> The cell was so small that I could stand in one place and touch both walls simultaneously. The ceiling was so low that I could reach up and touch the hot light fixture.
>
> My bed took up the length of the cell, and there was no other furniture at all … the walls were solid steel and painted all white.
>
> I was permitted to wear underwear, but I was given no other clothing. Shortly after I arrived, the prison staff began construction on the side pocket cell, adding more bars and other security measures to the cell while I was within it …
>
> It is hard to describe the horror I experienced during this construction process. As they built new walls around me it felt like I was being buried alive. It was terrifying.[55]

After reading such wretched tales from inmates about deplorable conditions, we should remember to keep certain things in mind. The absence of a federal death penalty makes solitary confinement the only option for inmates serving life sentences who repeatedly kill again while confined, especially those who murder staff.

The Quakers, who established the first penitentiary in 1790, and John Augustus, who first established probation some thirty years later, both had the same goal in mind. They were trying to reform drunkards and other social misfits committing mostly petty crimes and thus designed a method and a facility meant to deal primarily with these types of offenders. Today's super-max facilities, as well as prisons in general, are meant to serve an entirely different inmate population and must have a new mission and purpose, regardless of how it may betray the original intent of reformers.

The most important thing to remember is that inmates aren't assigned arbitrarily to super-max facilities to be singled out for specific rule violations. Inmates have to work very hard for the distinction. Out of a federal inmate population of about 219,000 in 2014, only about 490 are in the ADMAX facility. Among those inmates are foreign terrorists like Zacarias Moussaoui, who pleaded guilty to playing a key role in the September 11 attacks. Other Al-Qaeda operatives include Ramzi Yousef and Mahmud Abouhalima, who were convicted in connection with the 1993 World Trade Center bombings, plus Richard Reid, the notorious Al-Qaeda "shoe bomber."

One way of looking at super-max facilities is that they are prisons for the prison population community. Many inmates will tell staff that they're happy the Bureau of Prisons provides a place to keep dangerous predators away from them.

With 490 inmates in federal super max out of a population of 219,000, this comes to an incarceration rate of about 224 per 100,000. This is considerably lower than the US incarceration rate of 738 per 100,000—and lower than the top ten countries' incarceration rates that critics constantly quote to criticize our nation's criminal justice policies.

Charles H. Logan, a criminal justice researcher, describes a new mission for prisons. He calls it "the confinement model," and it is more realistic for the twenty-first century:

> It should be noted that under the confinement model offenders are sent to prison as punishment, not for punishment … Coercive confinement carries with it an obligation to meet the basic needs of prisoners at a reasonable standard of decency. Thus, measures of health care, safety, sanitation, nutrition, and other aspects of basic living conditions are relevant. Furthermore confinement must meet constitutional standards of fairness and due process. In short, confinement is much more than just warehousing.

He goes on to state what I think is the most important aspect of a new mission for prisons.

> Under the confinement model, a prison does not need to
> justify itself as a tool of rehabilitation or crime control
> or any other instrumental purpose at which an army of
> critics will forever claim it to be a failure.[56]

Under the confinement model, security, safety, and order are three of most important standards for prisons. This conforms to the basic premise of community policing and community justice.

An important aspect of the confinement model that must be noted is that confinement is much more than warehousing. Opportunities for education and vocational training as well as other services such as drug treatment and counseling should be made available.

In the BOP ADMAX, inmates are still allowed limited communication through phone calls and visits. Educational programs are broadcast into the inmates' cells via television, and they're allowed a variety of reading material. The type of inmates confined and the overall management and mission is what differentiates the isolation practices of the Walnut Street Jail from ADMAX. The former was designed to save people's souls and thus save people from themselves. The latter was designed to save other people's lives by protecting others from those who would prey on them. That's an important distinction that's lost on many reformers.

Partly because of ADMAX, where the most violent and dangerous inmates can be isolated from the rest of the population and for other reasons, homicides within BOP facilities have taken a nosedive. Many states have also built their own super-max facilities and have instituted other innovations. Consequently, our prisons are more peaceful than thirty-five years ago.

This has happened despite a surge of the prison population and severe overcrowding, contrary to what the experts have long predicted and warned us about. Better staff training and inmate classification systems have dramatically decreased prison homicides. Between 1980 and 2003, the state prison homicide rate dropped from 54.0 per 100,000 inmates to an astounding 5.7 per 100,000. This should strike inmate advocates as good news, but they persist in condemning prisons as if nothing has changed since the 1971 Attica riot.

During the first six years of my career with the Bureau of Prisons, each maximum-security penitentiary averaged around five inmate homicides a year. This was at time when the federal inmate population was about seven times smaller than its present size. Today, the entire bureau doesn't average that many inmate homicides in a year. During the period that I worked with the BOP (1973–2000), twelve federal correctional personnel were killed on duty, making it the deadliest era for staff in bureau history.

In May 1979, the Atlanta Federal Penitentiary experienced its twelfth inmate murder in thirty months. Primarily because of the high number of inmate homicides, congress had initiated hearings to investigate problems. Consequently, a new management system, pioneered by the BOP, was recommended for immediate implementation in Atlanta. Known as the Unit Management System, it divides the institution into several semiautonomous units. Each unit consists of a unit manager, two case managers, two correctional counselors, and a unit secretary. The unit offices are located in the inmate living units. The biggest problem with the big, fortress-like penitentiaries was that their sheer size made them very hard to manage and control.

In 1978, I was transferred to the Atlanta penitentiary as a case manager as part of unit management implementation. My office was a vacated inmate cell in one of the cellblocks. Instead of the inmates making an appointment to see their case manager or counselor in a more secure part of the institution, the inmates had ready access to us in their living quarters.

Better architectural design of facilities has also made Attica-type uprisings virtually a thing of the past. The old institutions were built with cube-shaped cellblocks enclosed within a boundary wall. This design contained dozens of blind spots where officers couldn't see any activities unless they walked up to a particular spot.

In the 1970s, the Federal Bureau of Prisons pioneered a new design for jails called "direct supervision." The direct supervision concept was designed for jails, but it was based on principles that the BOP considered vital for all correctional facilities, such as unit management.

The important distinction between prisons and jails is that jails are primarily temporary holding facilities for those awaiting trial or sentencing or otherwise serving short (less than one year) sentences. Length of stays in a jail can be measured in terms of hours and days, instead of years, as people are constantly released on bail or "time served." A jail's population is in constant flux, and this presents some unique problems.

Jail inmates aren't there long enough for much effective treatment or other activities. The relative idleness creates more opportunities for negative behaviors to surface. This in turn effects the entire institutional environment. A typical traditional jail atmosphere in many jurisdictions could be described as follows:

> There is an overpowering smell in the air of urine, sweat, stale food and Pine-sSol. Dirty, graffitied walls and littered floors of grey concrete with steel bar doors, remind one of zoo cages designed to be washed down with a hose. Blaring TV, banging doors, yelling men, make the noise deafening. Most of the inmates are young and have been there before. This is their turf. A few wander about, obviously mentally ill. The few uniformed officers remain secure behind a row of bars. One occasionally hurries in and out of this area on some mission, but little eye contact or personal contact is established.[57]

Notice that the environment described above is very similar to the street conditions of major cities with crime and disorder problems in the 1970s and 1980s. This is also the image of jails and prisons engraved in the public's mind by movies, TV shows, and written accounts. Now contrast that image with this one:

> A sunlit room with carpeted floors, attractive, soft furniture covered with fabrics of muted greys combined with bright blues and reds. Men joke around ordinary card tables while playing checkers. In a corner, several watch TV while sitting on an upholstered couch. The uniformed officer strolls by and stops to chat. An inmate asks her to open the door to his room so he can use the toilet. The room has a bed, sink, desk with desk lamp, and window with a view of the city street below.[58]

The first scene describes most of our nation's jails in the late twentieth century, including the infamous Manhattan jail, The Tombs. It was described as dangerous, unhealthy, and uncontrollable and was closed by a federal court order in 1974.

The Tombs was subsequently renovated and resurrected as a direct supervision jail and now more closely resembles the second description above. This model has now spread throughout the American correctional system, especially throughout the county jail system.

Direct supervision borrows heavily from the principles of Crime Prevention Through Environmental Design, or CPTED (pronounced sep-ted). CPTED focuses on creating crime-free environments in public places, and direct supervision strives for the same thing at the institution level. The institution is divided into manageable units each with its own staff. The cells are arranged in a circular configuration around a central day room. This eliminates the dangerous blind spots found in the linear design, where illegal activities and violence often occur. There are no physical barriers, such as enclosed booths, between officers and inmates.

Direct supervision principles were designed for jails but can be, and are, applied to prisons. What drives the concept is the notion of the institution as a community. The focus is on managing the environment rather than on controlling the inmates. One might say it's a microcosm of community policing in prison and jail. Officers are in constant and direct contact with inmates and get to know them so they can respond to trouble before it escalates into violence. Negotiation and communication become more important staff skills than brute strength.

Because jails are primarily temporary holding facilities, they're more susceptible to certain activities. Vandalism is more common because of the constant turnover of the population. More suicides occur in jails than in prisons. The negative effects of shock and depression are fresher in the mind during the initial hours or days after arrest.

Direct supervision jails tend to be virtually free from vandalism. After building a direct supervision jail in Pima County, Arizona, for example, the number of damaged mattresses dropped from 150 per year to none in two years; from an average of two TVs needing repair per week to two in two years; and from an average of ninety-nine sets of inmate clothes destroyed per week to fifteen sets in two years.[59]

Violence is also greatly reduced. The astounding drop in jail suicides mentioned in an earlier chapter is in no small part because of more direct supervision jails. Compared to traditional jails of similar size, direct supervision jails report much less conflict among inmates and between inmates and staff. Violent incidents are reduced 30 percent to 90 percent, and homosexual rape virtually disappears. [60]

Despite this great news, critics continue to focus on the violence and overcrowded conditions of our nation's prisons and jails. The most important consideration—staff and inmate safety—is ignored, and there's no universally accepted dominant measure of "overcrowded."

Prisons and jails are microcosms of society at large. The citizens in these communities deserve the same basic consideration to live without fear in a safe and secure environment. As in all communities, the most violent predators should be removed and incapacitated to keep them from endangering and preying upon the general population. Careful classification and institutional due process should weed out the most dangerous individuals and place them in more structured settings within the institution.

New and ever-changing conditions in society require new and innovative operating practices. Critics nonetheless continue to malign prisons for failing to perform the mission imposed on them by religious zealots more than two hundred years ago. Because of this, corrections in general and prisons in particular have suffered from a kind of identity crisis. This crisis was, and still remains in some jurisdictions, demonstrated in a vague or even contradicting sense of mission. Charles H. Logan states:

> We ask an awful lot of our prisons. We ask them to correct the incorrigible, rehabilitate the wretched, deter the determined, restrain the dangerous, and punish the wicked. We ask them to take over where other institutions of society have failed and reinforce the norms that have been violated and rejected. We ask them to pursue so many different and often incompatible goals that they seemed doomed to fail. Moreover when we lay upon prisons the utilitarian goals of rehabilitation, deterrence, and incapacitation, we ask them to achieve results primarily outside of prison, rather than inside.[61]

Reformers, however, tend to be offender but, more specifically, prisoner advocates. Their primary goal is to reduce, if not altogether eliminate, incarceration except for the "most violent" offenders. In their view, prisons are too harsh and have strayed from their "true" mission of rehabilitation.

The key question remains. What is the "true" purpose of not only the prison system but also the entire criminal justice system? Prisons are gaining a new sense of identity with a clear sense of mission and purpose. The prisons of today are radically different from the days of the Attica uprising. Innovative practices such as unit management, institutional design, direct supervision as well as better inmate classification methods and better-trained staff have made them less dangerous and more manageable.

Rather than rejoice in this good news, prison reformers continue to call prisons a dismal failure even though they are the very opposite

This begs an interesting question. If prison reformers really care about improving prison conditions, why don't they ever acknowledge and celebrate the truly positive reforms of the last three decades? The narrative of challenging an immoral and dysfunctional system seems better suited to their mission.

CONCLUSION

The history of the American criminal justice system is one of continuous reform. This may come as a surprise to some because the cries for reform seem to grow louder with time. This gives the impression that the system ignores the calls of reformers and is more concerned with perpetuating the system's abuses. Reformers demand changes to a system they describe as unjust, overly punitive, and riddled with racism and barbaric treatment of prison inmates.

The U.S. constitution was, and is, perhaps the most radical and revolutionary document ever written. For the first time in human history a free people declared themselves the masters of the governing authority because they were endowed with natural rights not bestowed by the government and therefore could not be denied by government. This was the foundation for structuring the American criminal justice system.

The penitentiary was itself a reform of traditional methods of punishment. American Quakers believed that deviants were sinners needing reform through penance. The mission of transforming law-breakers into responsible citizens was thrust upon our correctional system. Our courts concentrated on the individual offender's rights to due process more than on the rights of victims and on community safety and order. Reforming the police resulted in them shifting their focus from crime prevention and community wellbeing to responding to individual calls for assistance.

In the late twentieth and early twenty-first centuries it became increasingly clear that the old paradigm of justice wasn't suited for the growing disorder and crime in our communities. The system's operating procedures had in fact contributed to some of the problems. The police were the first to realize that a radical transformation was needed in their methods of accomplishing their mission. The other justice components began to follow the lead of the police but a larger question arose. What exactly was the mission of the criminal justice system?

In 1993 a group of scholars met to discuss new performance measures for the criminal justice system. Known as the Princeton study group, they came up with four "civic ideals" to define the purpose of the criminal justice system. The first ideal listed was "Doing Justice". The other three were Promoting secure communities, restoring crime victims, and promoting noncriminal options.

John Dilulio, a member of the study group explains each.

> Doing justice implies at least four things: hold offenders fully accountable for their offenses, protect offenders' constitutional and legal rights, treat like offenses alike, and take into account relevant differences among offenders and offenses.
>
> Promoting secure communities means more than to achieve low crime rates. Rather, it means providing the security to life, liberty, and property that is necessary for communities to flourish.
>
> Restoring victims means to honor the community's obligation to make victims of crime and disorder whole again.
>
> Finally, promoting noncriminal options means that punishment for criminal behavior should interfere as little as possible with the pursuit of noncriminal behavior.[62]

In essence, this became a new framework for the mission of criminal justice. As a result, the justice system has been transformed into serving the public's interest rather than being dedicated to actions for or against offenders and processing cases.

This transformation has occurred because the justice system took actions to change its operating practices rather than because new laws dictated any changes. By contrast, the reform movement is still engaged in working through the traditional political process of trying to pass, repeal, or amend laws. Because of this, the experts in the reform movement seem to be unaware of the transformation that's occurred and continues to grow beyond their awareness or understanding. Their frame of reference, which has been their foundation for so long, is completely different.

When I worked at NIC we were in Vermont observing a community reparative board. The board consists of citizens from the community hearing cases on juvenile offenses. The offender is brought to speak before the board and citizen observers. Board members determine reparations to the community and the victim. This keeps a lot of cases out of the traditional justice process and allows the community to be directly involved. This is all done under the authority of the probation department.

Among the observers of this process was a group of officials for agencies that are involved in criminal justice reform. Everyone was highly impressed and one person suggested to the reparative board members that the way to "sell" this program to the public was to tell them it was tough on crime (after all, this is what the public want's to hear).

I informed this individual that the group he was addressing *was* the public. He seemed somewhat taken aback and a bit confused. This spoke volumes. This bottom-up approach to changing the system defied his traditional top-down vision of reform.

The fact that this person referred to the reparative board as a program is also revealing. Just about all reform efforts focus on trying to implement the latest program (the ones that supposedly reduce incarceration). If one program works in one state it's assumed that it'll work in all states. The criminal justice transformation is not about merely implementing more of the latest programs. It's about implementing new strategies. This strategic view to solving problems is what makes this transformative rather than merely reformative. This defines the quiet revolution.

At the beginning of this book I said I wouldn't focus on the controversy of whether the police are becoming too militarized because of all the military hardware and tactics they've acquired and adopted. I'd like to mention something that too many people are never made aware of. While writing the conclusion to this book I came across a news story that to me illustrates problem oriented/solving policing at its best.

A police officer pulled over a mother and her five-year-old daughter because the girl wasn't in a car seat. The officer learned that the woman's car was actually repossessed earlier that day along with her daughter's booster seat, which was inside the vehicle. Instead of writing the woman a ticket, the officer met the family at Wal-Mart and purchased the little girl a booster seat.

The officer understood the true nature of the problem and knew that a ticket wouldn't help, but only worsen, the situation. The officer received much deserved praise and recognition for his service.

There's another lesson. The officer in the story could very well have been dressed in a military-style battle dress uniform (BDU) or "fatigues" as many tend to do nowadays. This wouldn't have made his actions any less compassionate. The most appalling examples of terrible policing can be found in pictures and films about the civil rights protests in the old south in the 1950's and 1960's. The cops demonstrated their rotten core to the world through their cruel and callous practices as they clubbed peaceful men, women, and young people. They did this while wearing their "class A" uniforms and without any armored vehicles or military equipment.

Good, as well as appalling, policing is a matter of the heart and not the skin. We should remember this before rendering judgement.

Many people ask me why I chose my particular profession and what made me remain in it. I'd like to end with one final story.

One morning while on my way to the Washington DC metro for my morning commute. I heard somebody calling me. "Mr. Barajas!" "Mr. Barajas!"

I turned and saw an ex-inmate that was on my caseload at the Lewisburg penitentiary running towards me. He came up to me and told me he wanted to shake my hand and thank me for encouraging him to enroll in a computer course at Lewisburg. He had been out several years and had a family and a great career in the high tech world. He was on his way to work.

It's moments like these that remind me why I enjoyed my career so much and why I never got discouraged. It's these same moments that remind me how wrong the critics of our criminal justice and prison systems are and why I needed to write this book.

The criminal justice system is progressing with a new sense of mission and purpose and it's time for everyone to recognize this. Mission clarity and moral clarity go hand in hand.

NOTES

[1] http://www.fbi.gov/about-us/cjis/ucr/crime-in-the-u.s/2012/crime-in-the-u.s.-2012/tables/1tabledatadecoverviewpdf/table_1_crime_in_the_united_states_by_volume_and_rate_per_100000_inhabitants_1993-2012.xls

[2] http://www.gallup.com/poll/144272/nearly-americans-fear-walking-alone-night.aspx

[3] http://thechairmansblog.gallup.com/2013_05_01_archive.html

[4] Bureau of Justice Statistics, Prisoners in 2012-Advance Counts, July 2013.

[5] McDonough, Siobhan. April 25, 2005. *Houston Chronicle*.

[6] Justice groups on right, left give road map for fixing TN, September16, 2014. *The Tennessean*.

[7] U.S. Department of Justice, http://www.justice.gov/ag/speeches/2010/ag-speech-100212.html

[8] Right on Crime, http://www.rightoncrime.com/the-conservative-case-for-reform/statement-of-principles/

[9] Bureau of Justice Statistics, Corrections Populations in the United States, December 2013.

[10] Stewart, James K. "Urban Crime Locks People in Poverty," Harvard Courant, July 15, 1986.

[11] Van Biema, David. May 14, 1984. Society Doesn't Cause Crime, Says Dr. Stanton E. Samenow; Criminals Do Because They Enjoy it. http://www.people.com/people/archive/article/0,,20087803,00.html

[12] US Department of Justice, In 1991, 45% of all state prisoners—or an estimated 327,000 offenders were sentenced to more than 1 year for violent offenses **(table 3)**. On December 31, 2006 (the year in which admissions to state prisons reached their peak), 50% of all sentenced prisoners in custody of state correctional authorities were violent offenders. In 2011 (the most recent year for which state prison offense data are available), more than 53% (or an estimated 718,000 offenders) of the year end population was serving a sentence for a violent crime. While robbery was the most com-

mon offense across the 20-year period, the proportion of violent offenders convicted for murder or any sexual assault increased over time. Property offenders (250,000 prisoners or 19% of all state prisoners) exceeded the number of drug offenders in custody in 2011 (223,000 inmates, or 17% of the inmate population. Bureau of Justice Statistics, Prisoners in 2012, Trends in Admissions and Releases, December 2013.

[13] Boaz, David. CATO Institute, Obama's New Drug Strategy, May 12, 2010

[14] Bureau of Justice Statistics, "Report to the Nation on Crime and Justice", March 1988.

[15] Bureau of Justice Statistics, "Mortality in Local Jails And State Prisons, 2000-2010-statistical Tables", December 13, 2012.

[16] Krause, Mike. "Prison Costs Are Running Out of Control: Start with Cutting Drug Sentences," Denver Post, June 26, 2005

[17] Susan Williams, "Report: Prison Costs Hurting Education," Charleston Gazette (West Virginia), May 15, 2005.

[18] "Prisons Eat Up Tax Dollars", Wisconsin State Journal (Madison), January 27, 2005.

[19] Bureau of Justice Statistics, "State Corrections Expenditures, FY 1982-2010."

[20] Schneider, Chelsea. 2014. Indiana reforms could push greater costs on counties. *Evansville Courier & Press.*

[21] Bureau of Justice Statistics, Homicide Trends in the United States, 1980-2008, November 2011.

[22] Bureau of Justice Statistics, Arrest in the United States, 1980-2009, September 2011.

[23] Ibid.

[24] Langan, Charles H, Dilulio, John J. Jr, Ten Myths about Crime and Prisons, Wisconsin Interest, Winter/Spring 1992.

[25] Myfoxdc.com, Greek prison system collapsing-labeled "inhuman", Associated Press, Dec. 30, 2013.

[26] Wikipedia, List of Countries by Incarceration Rates, http://en.wikipedia.org/wiki/Incarceration_rate

[27] Lovett, Ian. Court gives California More Time to Ease Prison Crowding, The New York Times, February 10, 2014.

[28] Wikipedia,http://en.wikipedia.org/wiki/Deinstitutionalisation

[29] Kelling, George L, Coles, Catherine M. Fixing Broken Windows, 1997.

[30] Kelling, George L, Wilson, James Q. Broken Windows, http://www.theatlantic.com/magazine/archive/1982/03/broken-windows/304465/ Kelling and Wilson described the effects of New Jersey's "Safe and Clean Neighborhoods Program" which consisted of, among several things, getting police officers out of cars and walking beats. The results concluded that while the program didn't reduce crime, fear of crime was greatly reduced in those neighborhoods with foot pa-

trols. The police officers on the beat also reported greater job satisfaction and a more favorable attitude toward citizens than those assigned to patrol cars.

[31] MacDonald, Heather. Is the Criminal-Justice System Racist? *City Journal.* Spring 2008.

[32] Langan, Patrick A. America's Soaring Prison Population, *Science Magazine*, March 29, 1991.

[33] Calandro, Lisa, Reeder, Dennis J, Cormier, Karen. Evolution of DNA Evidence for Crime Solving - A Judicial and Legislative History, *Forensic Magazine*, Jan. 6 2005.

[34] Kelling, George, Coles, Catherine M. Fixing Broken Windows, Simon and Schuster Inc., 1996.

[35] Ibid.

[36] No Remorse in Spree Suspect Cops Say Royster is Cold Customer, *New York daily News.* June 15, 1996.

[37] MacDonald, Heather. Emptying NY Prisons, *New York Post*, March 12, 2013.

[38] Rothwax, Harold J. Guilty. The Collapse of Criminal Justice, Warner Books, 1996.

[39] Ibid.

[40] Reynolds, M.O.Using the Private Sector to Deter Crime, the National Center for Policy Development, 1994.

[41] Kay, Judith S. Chief Judge, State of New York. 1996. Center for Court Innovation, Midtown Community Court Video. http://www.courtinnovation. org/topic/community-court

[42] Ibid.

[43] Center for Court Innovation. Red Hook Community Justice Center Video. http:// www.courtinnovation.org/research/red-hook-community-justice-center-vide o?url=research%2F4%2Fvideo&mode=4&type=video

[44] Ibid.

[45] Ibid.

[46] American Prosecutors Research Institute. Community Prosecution. A Guide for Prosecutors. 1993

[47] Ibid.

[48] McKinley, James Jr. In Unusual Collaboration, Police and Prosecutors Team Up to Reduce Crime, *New York Times*, June 4, 2014.

[49] Center for Court Innovation Website, Denver's Community Justice Councils. http://www.courtinnovation.org/research/denver's-community-justice-councils

[50] Lardner, George Jr. The Stalking of Kristen, New York: *Atlantic Monthly Press*, 1995.

[51] American Probation and Parole Association, Position Statement on Community Justice, January 2000.

52 Jordan, James T. Boston's Operation Night Light. New roles, new rules. *FBI Law Enforcement Bulletin*. Volume 67. Number 8. August 1998.

53 Ibid.

54 Biggs, Brooke Shelby. Solitary Confinement: A Brief History. *Mother Jones*, March 2, 2009.

55 Casella, Jean and Rideway, James. America's Most Isolated Federal Prisoner Describes 10,220 Days in Extreme Solitary Confinement, *Solitary Watch*, May 5, 2011.

56 Logan, Charles H. Performance Measures for the Criminal Justice System, U.S. Department of Justice, Office of Justice Programs, Bureau of Justice Statistics, October 1993.

57 Warner, Richard, Frazier, F.W., Farbstein, Jay. Direct Supervision of Correctional Institutions, *Podular, Direct Supervision Jails Info Packet*, National Institute of Corrections, 1993.

58 Ibid.

59 Ibid.

60 Ibid.

61 Charles H. Logan, Performance Measures for the Criminal Justice System, U.S. Department of Justice, Office of Justice Programs, Bureau of Justice Statistics, October 1993.

62 Dilulio, John J. Jr, Performance Measures for the Criminal Justice System, U.S. Department of Justice, Office of Justice Programs, Bureau of Justice Statistics, October 1993.

GLOSSARY

Community Corrections: Also called "alternatives to incarceration" by some. Community corrections centers/halfway houses, probation, and parole fall under the heading of community corrections. This applies to people serving their sentence in the community rather than a prison or jail. Individuals serving the last months of their sentence or an entire short sentence in a CTC are listed as inmates and may thus artificially inflate the numbers of prisoners in prison

Community Corrections Centers/Facilities: Also called halfway houses, these are facilities that assist inmate transition from prison into the community. These facilities are, for the most part, operated by private entities such as the Volunteers of America (VOA), but some corrections departments may also contract with sheriffs departments to use county work-release facilities (see jails) as halfway houses for inmates. Many private halfway houses are former single-family homes in urban neighborhoods.

The Federal Bureau of Prisons transfers the vast majority of inmates to halfway houses, or community corrections centers (CCC), during the last six months of their sentence. Inmates can also serve an entire short sentence of up to six months in a CCC if they meet certain requirements regarding the nature of the offense or the need for particular treatment or consideration. CCC staff assists inmates in finding employment and suitable housing and can provide other services, such as drug treatment.

Probationers and parolees can also be placed in these facilities as a condition of probation or parole if it is felt the individual needs more intensive supervision or is homeless.

Correctional System: The correctional system refers to the federal and state authorities responsible for supervising convicted individuals either in secure facilities, such as jails and prisons, in the community under probation and parole, or in community facilities, such as halfway houses.

Courts: The courts are responsible for holding hearings and trials of offenders charged with committing an offense and sentencing those who are found guilty. Courts also issue warrants to help investigate criminal activities. Courts handle criminal trials as well as conduct civil hearings for lawsuits and other civil disputes.

Judges are the highest court officials. The judicial system can range from municipal to county and state as well as federal court systems. In several systems, including the federal system, judges are appointed by the chief executive of the state or by the president of the United States. In other systems, judges run for office and are elected.

Jails: County detention facilities meant to temporarily house pretrial and presentenced inmates, or those serving less than one-year sentences. Jails may have satellite work-release facilities, which are minimum-security facilities where inmates reside but perform work in the community. Jail programs can also include such things as electronic monitoring for certain low-risk inmates. This allows them to reside in the community while wearing an electronic monitoring device around the ankle or wrist.

Parole: Provisional release from prison under obligation to the state. A person can be eligible for parole consideration after service of a certain portion of his or her sentence. Parole boards my take into account the inmate's behavior while in prison, the severity of the offense, and other factors prior to granting parole. If granted, a person can serve the remaining portion of a sentence in the community rather than in prison.

As is the case with probationers, parolees live in the community under certain conditions and are supervised by parole officers. Parole officers assist inmates in making the transition from prison to freedom. If the conditions of parole are violated, parole may be revoked and the individual returned to prison to serve the remainder of the sentence or placed in more restricted programing in the community.

The organizational structure of parole varies among jurisdictions. The parole board, which decides whether to grant or revoke parole, may be an independent agency appointed by the governor, while the parole department may be within a state department of probation and parole. Some states and the federal government discontinued parole as part of tougher sentencing policies enacted in the 1980s and early 1990s.

Police: The police are state and local law-enforcement professionals whose job is to patrol our streets and investigate criminal activity and apprehend suspects. There are about eighteen thousand state and local police departments in the United States.

Although there are federal law-enforcement agencies and officers, technically there is no federal police force. Federal agents investigate crimes covered by federal law, such as bank robbery, and any crimes that occur over state lines, such as kidnapping a person in one state and transporting them to another, and apprehend such suspects.

Local police are primarily municipal or city law enforcement but can include county police and county sheriffs departments. In a few counties, the county sheriff has no policing duties, such as patrolling the streets, but the department is responsible for such functions as running the jail, court security, and serving warrants.

Prisons: State and federal detention facilities designed to house inmates serving sentences of more than one year up to life or awaiting execution in those jurisdictions with the death penalty. The federal system and states have adopted a classification system that ranks prisons from minimum security to maximum and, in some jurisdictions, super-maximum security. Different criteria are used across jurisdictions to determine the security level but most commonly have to do with perimeter security (type of fence or wall), housing units (dormitories or cells), and relative freedom allowed inmates within the compound (free movement except during lights out or security counts, confinement to cells except during certain periods of time, or up to twenty-plus hours of time confined in cells).

The Federal Bureau of Prisons is known in professional circles as the BOP. The BOP is the federal agency responsible for all federal prisons housing inmates convicted of federal crimes. Such crimes range from white-collar crimes, such as tax evasion and stock fraud, to violent offenses, such as bank robbery. Any crime committed on federal property or is involved across state lines is considered a federal crime, which gives most offenses, including murder and rape, the possibility of becoming federal cases. The federal system also prosecutes large-scale drug importing and distribution networks as well as any large-scale interstate criminal organizations.

The National Institute of Corrections (NIC) is an autonomous institution within the BOP that was established to provide training and technical assistance to state and local corrections and justice agencies. It consists of a director and an assistant director. The Prisons Division and the Community Corrections Division are in Washington DC. The Jails Division, the National Academy of Corrections, and the Corrections Information Center are in Longmont, Colorado.

Probation: A sentencing option meant to be an alternative to incarceration. A person can be sentenced to probation for a set period of time and remain at home and continue normal activities within certain restrictions imposed by the court, such as refraining from using illegal drugs or alcohol. Probationers are supervised by probation officers who periodically check their progress and compliance either through the probationer reporting to the probation office or the officer visiting the individual in his or her home.

Probation departments differ in organizational structure. In some states and in the federal system, probation is under the courts. In some states, probation is under the state corrections department or it can be a function of the county government. Some large cities, such as New York, have city probation departments.

Prosecution: The act of prosecuting crimes and the system responsible for its functioning. A prosecutor is an elected official of a county or a designated district responsible for prosecuting crimes. The duties include investigating alleged crimes in cooperation with law enforcement and filing criminal charges or bringing evidence before the grand jury that may lead to an indictment for a crime. The chief prosecutor in most states is called a district attorney, but in some states, they're referred to as a county attorney or a state's attorney.

At the federal level, the president appoints United States attorneys who are prosecutors for districts (there are several in larger states) within the US Department of Justice.

BIBLIOGRAPHY

American Probation and Parole Association, http://appa.org

Barajas, Eduardo. 1995. Moving Toward Community Justice. *Community Justice: Striving for Safe, Secure, and Just Communities*: Page 1-7. https://s3.amazonaws.com/static.nicic.gov/Library/013227.pdf

Bureau of Justice Statistics, http://www.bjs.gov

Bureau of Justice Statistics, Performance Measures for the Criminal Justice System, http://www.bjs.gov/content/pub/pdf/pmcjs.pdf

Center for Court Innovation, http://www.courtinnovation.org

City Journal, http://www.city-journal.org

Federal Bureau of Investigation, http://www.fbi.gov

Federal Bureau of Prisons, http://www.bop.gov

Forensic Magazine, Evolution of DNA Evidence for Crime Solving - A Judicial and Legislative History, January 6, 2005.

Kelling, George L. Coles, Catherine M. Fixing Broken Windows, Restoring Order and Reducing Crime in our Communities. New York, NY: Touchstone, 1997

MacDonald, Heather. *Are Cops Racist? How the war against the police harms Black Americans*, Chicago, IL: Ivan R. Dee, 2003.

Manhattan Institute for Policy Research, http://www.manhattan-institute.org

Moses, Kenneth R. 2010. Automated Fingerprint Identification System (AFIS). *Fingerprint Sourcebook* NCJ225326: Chapter 6. https://www.ncjrs.gov/App/Publications/abstract.aspx?ID=247306

National District Attorneys Association, http://www.ndaa.org

National Institute of Corrections, http://nicic.gov

Rothwax, Harold J. Guilty, *The Collapse of Criminal Justice*, New York, NY: Warner Books, 1996.

TRUE DIRECTIONS
An affiliate of Tarcher Books

OUR MISSION

Tarcher's mission has always been to publish books
that contain great ideas. Why? Because:

GREAT LIVES BEGIN WITH GREAT IDEAS

At Tarcher, we recognize that many talented authors, speakers,
educators, and thought-leaders share this mission and deserve to be
published – many more than Tarcher can reasonably publish ourselves.
True Directions is ideal for authors and books that increase awareness,
raise consciousness, and inspire others to live their ideals and passions.

Like Tarcher, True Directions books are designed to do three things:
inspire, inform, and motivate.

Thus, True Directions is an ideal way for these important voices to
bring their messages of hope, healing, and help to the world.

Every book published by True Directions– whether it is non-fiction, memoir,
novel, poetry or children's book – continues Tarcher's mission to publish works
that bring positive change in the world. We invite you to join our mission.

For more information, see the True Directions website:
www.iUniverse.com/TrueDirections/SignUp

Be a part of Tarcher's community to bring positive change in this world!
See exclusive author videos, discover new and exciting books, learn about
upcoming events, connect with author blogs and websites, and more!
www.tarcherbooks.com

TRUE DIRECTIONS
AN AFFILIATE OF TARCHER BOOKS

www.ingramcontent.com/pod-product-compliance
Lightning Source LLC
Chambersburg PA
CBHW050406290526
45786CB00003B/1146